From Indian Island to Omaha Beach

The *D-Day* Story of Charles Shay

Penobscot Indian War Hero

Sample chapters from the forthcoming biography

to be published by University of Nebraska Press, 2020

Limited edition to commemorate

75th Anniversary of D-Day, 6 June 2019

Harald E.L. Prins & Bunny McBride

Wisbee Creek Press
Bath, Maine

Dedicated in the spirit of the sacred eagle feather
to North American Indian warriors
killed in the invasion of Normandy on D-Day 1944, including:

Nicholas Naganashe (Odawa) 16th Regt, 1st Infantry
Kenneth Fatty (Onondaga) 299th Eng. Combat Battalion
John Clifton (Cherokee) 116th Regt, 29th Infantry
Phillip Stands (Sicangu Lakota) 101st Airborne
Peter Black Cloud (Dakota) 82nd Airborne
Johnnie Rivas (Comanche) 82nd Airborne
Donald Cornbread (Washoe) 82nd Airborne
Chester Courville (Muckleshoot) 82nd Airborne
Charles Louis (Coeur d'Alene) 82nd Airborne
Turner Turnbull (Choctaw) 82nd Airborne[1]
Herman Stock (Mohawk) Queen's Own Rifles
Herman Hotomani (Nakota) Regina Rifles
Mathew Desjarlais (Saulteaux) Regina Rifles
William Pangman (Saulteaux) Royal Winnipeg Rifles
Phillip Genaille (Saulteaux) Royal Winnipeg Rifles
Charles Bird (Cree) Regina Rifles
Bill A. Daniels (Cree) Regina Rifles
Donald Thomas (Cree) Regina Rifles
Percy Dreaver (Cree) Regina Rifles
Thomas V. Bird (Cree) Royal Winnipeg Rifles
Russell Isbister (Cree) Royal Winnipeg Rifles
Jean Louis (Anishinaabe) Royal Winnipeg Rifles
Wilfred Nabish (Anishinaabe) Royal Winnipeg Rifles
Charles Doucette (Mi'kmaq) N. Nova Scotia Highlanders[2]

---

[1] Landed on D-Day, killed the following day.

[2] Taken prisoner on D-Day, executed the following day.

CONTENTS

Note: All chapters that will appear in the forthcoming full biography of Charles Norman Shay are listed here. Titles of sample chapters included in this volume are in bold font.

ACKNOWLEDGMENTS

Over the past dozen years, many people on both sides of the Atlantic have been helpful in various ways with the research resulting in this volume. Even more have helped with the forthcoming full-length biography from which these chapters are drawn. Personal acknowledgments will come with that larger book, expected to be published in 2020, when the end of the Second World War will be commemorated. For now, we offer broad-stroke but nonetheless deepfelt gratitude for support received from Kansas State University, the First Division Museum and the Maine Humanities Council, as well as individuals working for the Penobscot Indian Nation, the Passamaquoddy Tribe, the University of Nebraska Press, the American Battleground Memorial Commission, the Big Red One Museum (Normandy), UNESCO, École des Hautes Études en Sciences Sociales and Luxembourg's Ministry of Foreign Affairs.

INTRODUCTION

On my first return to Omaha Beach a decade ago, I made a small ceremonial fire and burned sacred tobacco and sweet grass near the place where I had struggled ashore. Fanning the smoke with a sacred eagle feather, I reached out to the spirits of those who died on that beach. Seeking peace, I prayed while the sweet-smelling smoke slowly rose, carrying my thoughts into the sky.

(Charles Norman Shay, "Fallen Warriors & Gold
Star Mothers: A Personal Reflection," 5 June 2017)[1]

From his home beside the Penobscot River on Indian Island in Maine, Charles Shay often sees white-headed eagles soaring above the falls nearby. Since time immemorial, this majestic bird has been sacred to indigenous peoples across North America. Its large tail and wing feathers are vital to their spiritual ceremonies. Thus, when Charles made his first pilgrimage from Indian Island back to Omaha Beach in October 2007, he carried with him an eagle feather (*nsawakani-awihpon* in Penobscot).

Omaha, a crescent-shaped beach extending eight kilometers along the Normandy coast, had been seared in Charles' memory on 6 June 1944 – "D-Day." At dawn on that cold cloudy day, he was baptized by fire as a 19-year-old combat medic attached to an assault platoon in the U.S. Army's 1st Infantry Division, known as the "Big Red One." The young Penobscot Indian struggled ashore from the stormy sea as part of the first wave of attack in Operation Neptune – the largest seaborne invasion in world history. He was unarmed, like other brave-hearted medics rushing from one wounded soldier to another amid exploding shrapnel and the strafing of enemy machine guns. Disregarding his own safety, he repeatedly returned to the tidal flat to rescue maimed soldiers from drowning in the rising sea. For his gallantry on that savage shore, he was awarded a Silver Star.

About 2,400 men became casualties at Omaha that day – drowned, killed or wounded. The foot soldier units that spearheaded the attack suffered the greatest losses. Charles' company in the 16th Infantry Regiment was decimated and lost all its officers by mid-day. Scattered and leaderless, soldiers still fit for battle joined other units as they fought their way up the bluffs.

Miraculously, not a single bullet or shred of shrapnel ripped into Charles' flesh as he worked amid the carnage. By late afternoon, drained and lost, he wandered across the beach, now littered with burning vehicles, mangled corpses and debris. Later finding his way to a trail up the bluffs, he lay down – "somewhere." Then, utterly exhausted and turning a deaf ear to the incessant blasts of artillery and the roaring engines of landing boats, tanks, bulldozers and trucks, he fell asleep under the open sky.

And so ended Charles' first day in battle. Over the next ten months or so, he witnessed the maiming and killing of many hundreds of fellow soldiers, rescuing as many as he could until he became a prisoner of war in Germany on 25 March 1945.

Years later, Charles learned that he was not the only Native American on that crescent beach. Among the 34,000 soldiers who landed on Omaha that day, about 175 were tribesmen hailing from a few dozen Indian reservations all across the United States. One of them, fellow Penobscot Melvin Neptune, who had already fought in North Africa and Sicily, heroically distinguished himself during his first night of combat in Normandy. After D-Day, seven more Penobscot tribesmen joined many thousands of other American and Canadian Indian soldiers in liberating France and neighboring countries from Nazi-German tyranny.

When Charles first returned to Normandy as an 83-year-old tribal Elder, we had the privilege of accompanying him (supported by grants from the Maine Humanities Council and the First Division Museum). Soon after we arrived, he quietly performed a ritual on Omaha Beach to honor fallen comrades. With his eagle feather, he fanned tobacco smoke over his face and body, purifying himself for the sacred act.

In the years since that private ceremony, Charles has dedicated himself to honoring fallen comrades in many ways. In particular, he has focused on drawing attention to the military service and sacrifices of fellow Penobscots and other Native Americans. In 2009, he took the initiative to push for official recognition of veterans belonging to Maine's four tribal communities. This resulted in the State of Maine officially designating 21 June as Native American Veterans Day – the first state in the county to establish such a day.

Building his cause, Charles has accepted many invitations to speak at ceremonies and other events where he talks about his tribal heritage and military experiences. He has spoken not only in the United States, but also in France, Germany – and Austria, which was his country of residence for decades after he met and married a Viennese woman during the Allies' post-war occupation of her homeland.

Among his illustrious ancestors, Charles takes pride in a seventeenth-century French baron who came to seacoast Maine as a military officer, became a wealthy fur trader and married the daughter of a famous Penobscot grand chief. True to this distinguished heritage, Charles has welcomed opportunities to connect with the French side of his ancestral heritage in the old southern province of Béarn, acting as an ambassador to rekindle French-Penobscot relations reaching back to their strategic alliance against English invaders during America's colonial era.

Beyond offering speeches and participating in ceremonies and cultural exchanges, Charles has put some of his life story in writing, publishing *Project Omaha Beach: The Life and Military Service of a Penobscot Indian Elder* (2012).

Since his first pilgrimage back to Omaha in 2007, Charles has returned to Normandy in early June almost every year to participate in D-Day commemorative events. While he was there in 2016 to speak at the Normandy American Memorial on D-Day, we decided to join him in spirit by walking the beach of his ancestral homeland on our side of the Atlantic. As we meandered along a stretch of the Maine coast, we thought of him – a man who likes to say, "the spirits are guiding" whenever something wondrous happens. And so it was that one of us noticed a large eagle feather floating on a wave rolling toward us. This was a sacred bird's gift to be shared. So, some months later, during one of Charles' visits at our home, we gave it to him. Holding the long feather that had dropped from an eagle as she flew above the coastal sea, Charles reflected on D-Day and the spirit world where he expects to rejoin those who once walked the earth in war and peace. The photograph on the front of this book was taken during that contemplation. Charles carried the feather back home to Indian Island. The following year Penobscot artist Jennifer Neptune created a beautiful color-beaded leather haft for the hollow shaft, and Charles ceremonially donated the sacred bird's feather to the Mémorial de Caen, a fitting gift to the French museum commemorating World War II while focusing on the fragility of peace.

Over the years, Charles has sought ways to honor individual WWII comrades, helping to secure medals for them and then traveling long distances to deliver the tributes. He has carried these to dying veterans and to the families of those who are no longer living. Among the latter is fellow combat medic Edward Morozewicz, who died the day both of them landed on Omaha Beach.

While paying tribute to others, Charles has become the recipient of numerous tributes himself. Within weeks of returning from his initial pilgrimage to Omaha Beach, he was honored by France's then President Nicolas Sarkozy, who personally inducted him into the Légion d'Honneur in a ceremony at the French ambassador's home in Washington. Next, Charles was inducted as a Distinguished Member of the 16th Regiment in a ceremony at Fort Riley, Kansas, home base of the 1st Infantry Division.

Perhaps the most enduring tribute born of Charles' efforts is a small memorial park created in Saint-Laurent-sur-Mer to honor all North American Indians who landed in Normandy on 6 June 1944 as part of the huge Allied invasion (primarily American, British and Canadian forces) to liberate Western Europe. The park came into being primarily thanks to French citizen Marie-Pascale Legrand. Moved by the ultimate sacrifice made by so many thousands of young foreign men buried in her homeland, she felt inspired to honor Charles as one of the last living WWII veterans. This commemorative ground, nestled in low dunes overlooking the middle of Omaha Beach, is named "The Charles Shay Indian Memorial." It is situated below the farmland where army doctors and nurses once treated severely-wounded soldiers in large army tents at the first American military field hospital erected just days after D-Day close to a newly-laid airstrip for "flying ambulances." The small park features a granite turtle carved by Charles' nephew Tim Shay (a sculptor and traditional spiritual leader) and a memorial plaque. The plaque, adorned with images of the eagle feather found on the Maine coast, offers a brief historic text and mentions by name some of the 175 American Indian soldiers who landed on Omaha Beach on D-Day. (So far, we have identified just over a third of those brave tribesmen. Among their numbers are individuals who were killed, wounded, captured and/or decorated for valor.)

Charles Shay Indian Memorial dedication. ©2017 Harald E.L. Prins

Charles' advocacy for Native American war veterans has utilized his natural gifts and prompted him to grow and expand in ways that few people do in the later chapters of their lives. He is now in his mid-nineties, and his tireless efforts are an inspiration. For us, it has been an honor – and a challenge – to track down information needed to support his goal of identifying and drawing attention to American Indian veterans. The effort has included combing historical materials in numerous libraries and archives (including the McCormick Research Center at the First Division Museum, collaborating with research historian Andrew Woods), scouring countless newspapers, finding and mining huge numbers of obituaries and cemetery records, and also locating and talking with survivors in the fast-shrinking pool of living veterans. Who knew there were about 6,000 individuals from scores of tribal nations training in the British Isles before the June 1944 invasion of Western Europe? Certainly, we didn't – until we began working with Charles. Even military historians specialized on D-Day and the Battle of Normandy missed the fact that more than 500 young warriors crossed the stormy sea in airplanes and aboard ships to fight in Normandy on D-Day.

Charles' story appealed to us because of that goal and also because he served as a medic, saving rather than taking human lives. Notably, his military career as a medic taps into deep ancestral roots: His great-grandmother, the daughter of a Penobscot tribal leader famous and feared for his mysterious spirit power, was a well-known traveling herbal doctress.

Medics like Charles were praised by fellow soldiers as "the bravest of the brave." Indeed, the number of personal decorations awarded to the medics in his regiment for their valor on D-Day was extraordinarily high: 54 Bronze Stars (six posthumously), 35 Silver Stars (three posthumously) and four Distinguished Service Crosses. Identified by the Red Cross symbol on their upper sleeve, they were supposedly protected by the Conventions of Geneva. Still, their casualties were high. On D-Day, 22 medics in the 16th Regiment were wounded, and eight were killed (five of whom are buried at the American Cemetery overlooking Omaha).

Currently, we are completing a hefty book-length biography about Charles. The slim volume in hand, printed in a limited edition to commemorate the 75th anniversary of D-Day, is comprised of relevant chapters excerpted from that forthcoming (2020) book. Charles' life story brings to light the mostly ignored or forgotten sacrifices made by North American Indian soldiers and their communities, not only on D-Day but also in the subsequent battles of Normandy, Aachen, Huertgen Forest, the Ardennes (Battle of the Bulge) and Rhineland, where he was captured toward the end of World War II. Woven into the narrative are emblematic stories of many other Native Americans who participated in the liberation of Europe.

Charles Shay's full biography, told partly in his own words, begins with his ancestors and moves through his growing up years on Indian Island, before he was drafted, went through basic training and then shipped out to England in preparation for Operation Neptune. After the WWII chapters, the story continues with several post-war military years in Vienna, where Charles met and married the love of his life. Then came his service in Japan and Korea during the Korean War when he was promoted to Master Sergeant and awarded three Bronze Stars for heroic frontline achievements. Soon after returning to his homeland, he joined the Air Force and served as a medic in a squadron dispatched to the Marshall Islands in the Pacific where nuclear bombs were tested. The final chapters cover his post-military years with his Austrian wife in Vienna, their return to Indian Island, her death and his remarkable emergence from grieving widower to tribal Elder activist.

PROLOGUE
Spirits on Omaha Beach

Charles tossed and turned, waiting for dawn. Wishing it would come. Wishing it wouldn't. Then, suddenly, he awoke. So, he must have slept after all. Rising, he washed and dressed with even greater care than usual. Everything had to be perfect for what he intended to do that day. Breakfast, served in the vast dining room of an ancient castle near France's Normandy seacoast, seemed beside the point. He ate without tasting. Picking up the bag he had packed for this long-anticipated day, he stepped out into the misty morning and climbed into the car that would take him to Omaha Beach. He felt old. He *was* old – eighty-three years, and then some.

An ocean away, on Indian Island, a tribal reservation village in Maine, his nephew and a small circle of Native friends sat in a smoke-filled canvas tepee. For them, morning light was still hours away and they were just midway through their night-long vigil of peyote songs, rituals and prayer. They sought power, guidance and healing – for him, Charles Norman Shay, an Elder in the Penobscot Indian Nation.

Approaching the beach, Charles followed the winding path that led from the cemetery through a tangle of trees and bushes down to the shore. He took his time, slowed by memories and the weight of his bag. It held firewood and the ritual paraphernalia required for the spiritual ceremony he had planned.

Charles came from a long line of Penobscot Indian leaders and had participated in many tribal performances and ceremonial events during his growing up years. Yet, he had never led a ceremony, for he had left his community as a

9

young man and had only recently returned there to live out his final years. Today, there would be no audience, but still, he felt anxious. All in all, it seemed a daunting undertaking, especially for an old combat medic who had resisted thinking about Omaha Beach since landing here as part of the biggest military invasion in human history on 6 June 1944 – D-Day.

Stepping onto the vast sandy beach, Charles encountered unexpected quiet. No roaring aircraft. No bursting mortar shells. No thunderous artillery fire. No wounded men screaming in agony. This time he could hear the sea. And the calls of gulls. Perhaps even the flapping of wings. He took a deep breath of salty sea air. It held no hint of battlefield smoke, diesel fuel or smoldering flesh.

On this cool October day, only a few distant people dotted the long pale beach. As Charles walked along the shore at high tide, he glanced back and forth from the sea on his left to the bluffs on his right. Where was the high embankment of tide-piled pebbles that had lined the shore six decades ago? Landing at incoming tide on D-Day, he had taken refuge behind that natural barrier after leaping from his landing craft, struggling through rough water and making his way up the beach – weaving around mined obstacles and fallen men as he stumbled forward. After regaining his senses, he had returned to the sea, lifted wounded comrades from the rising blood-stained surf, dragged them to the protective embankment and treated them as best he could with the basic supplies in his first-aid kit.

Protection provided by a pile of loose stones was a poor match for the firestorm raining down on Charles and the many men he saved – and failed to save – on that horrific day. He was just 19 years old, and it was his first combat experience. Now, so many years later, he found it difficult to imagine he had been in that bloodbath, even though he had been awarded a Silver Star for his heroic efforts.

Reaching the area he intuited to be about where he had come ashore and tended so many fallen comrades, Charles put down his sack. He took the kindling he had brought and arranged it for a small fire. Then, one by one, he pulled the consecrating items from the sack and placed them near the firewood: a large dark eagle feather, a braid of sweetgrass, a small bundle of sage, a leather pouch of rich brown tobacco. Each item had been gifted to him from individuals back home for this occasion. The tobacco came from a brother of Melvin Neptune, a fellow Penobscot who landed here on D-Day.

Removing his jacket, Charles looked down at the beaded deer-hide vest his nephew's Navajo wife had made for him to wear on this day. Its beauty encouraged him. He crouched down to light the fire. Slow to catch, it burned haltingly. But that was enough.

Standing as erect as possible, the old Indian veteran faced eastward, took a pinch of tobacco from the pouch, touched it to his forehead and then dropped it into the fire. Sparks flew up high and vanished in the air. He did the same in each of the other three directions. Then, bending over the flames, he picked up the eagle feather and used it to fan the tobacco smoke over his face and body, cleansing himself in the sacred haze. Next, he lit the sweetgrass and sage and purified himself in their scented smoke.

The wordless ritual hid the fullness of Charles' thoughts – his conversation with the young men who had taken their last breath here as they passed on to the spirit world: *I am showing you my respect. I know that soon I will be joining you – but my death will not be like yours was here, surrounded by the cruel chaos of combat.*

He could not help but also think of his mother, whose prayers had sustained him and his three brothers throughout the war. And the other woman in his life – his

Viennese wife Lilli, who he met during the post-war Allied occupation of Austria. In the autumn of their lives she had surrendered the familiar surroundings of her country, where they had lived so long and so happily, and moved to Indian Island with him. A year later, she had died.

It was a silent ceremony marking the end of six decades of silence. That evening he said, "Before planning my return to Omaha Beach, I had never discussed my experiences in 1944 with anyone, not even my wife. Just after the ceremony, I was in a very sad mood and took a few minutes to pray. This helped me to feel better. Then I covered the fire with sand. It had served its purpose. It gave me peace of mind."[2]

Charles' first ceremony on Omaha Beach, 3 Oct. 2007. ©Bunny McBride

CHAPTER 1
Foreshadowing

There was always a section of the Penobscot River that didn't freeze. The old tribal legend was that it was waiting to claim someone, and it always did. A grownup would walk over the ice at night and fall into an open place, or little kids out skating would suddenly tumble through thin ice and disappear. After snatching someone, the cold dark patch of water would glaze over, hiding its grim deed.

At age six, Charlie Shay put all 42 inches (106 cm) of his height toward saving his little brother Pat from the river's frigid clutch. "We were on our sleds having a good time," he recalled,

> propelling ourselves over the frozen river with ice picks that we made by pounding nails into the ends of sticks. We came to a place on the east side of Indian Island [near the falls] that doesn't freeze fully because of the current. Pat's sled went right through the ice and so did he. Robert Hamilton, a Penobscot boy a few years older than me,[3] happened to be walking across the river from Milford and saw me lying on the ice struggling to reach Pat. He ran over, lay down on his stomach, took hold of my feet and pushed me out so I could shove my sled closer to my brother. Pat grabbed it and we pulled him out.[4]

On an early December day, a decade after rescuing his brother, Charlie and his cousin Leslie Ranco heard the cries of another Penobscot boy who had fallen through the ice. Seven-year-old Boyd Thomas had crossed the river safely to Milford, but on his way back to Indian Island, the ice gave way about 6 meters from the shore. As Charles recollected, "Leslie and I grabbed a canoe and held onto it for safety as we began pushing it toward Boyd. But the ice was so thin I was afraid we'd break through, so I went back to shore. The boy drowned. It weighed heavy on me."[5]

Sometimes, in the final season of our lives, when we have lived long enough to gain perspective, we look back and see that certain childhood moments were full of portent. They take on special meaning because of something we do or some event we're involved in years later. There are several moments like that in Charles' growing up years – moments foreshadowing victory as well as defeat.

The childhood memories carried by Charles for nine decades come from the heart of the Penobscot Indian Nation reservation, a 315-acre island shaped like an arrowhead. Indian Island, as it is named, rises above tribal waters between Milford and Old Town, Maine, spread out on opposite banks of the Penobscot River. Until 1950, there was no bridge connecting the island village to either of these mainland towns. Because the island lies where the river widens, just above the rocky ledges of a great falls, Charles' ancestors referred to the place as *Panawahpskek* ("where the rocks spread out").

Charles will tell you that living entirely within a river's embrace is a far cry from living on one bank of a stream. When you are surrounded by water, it has enormous importance. For one thing, it puts you on your guard because it is unpredictable – sometimes easygoing and inviting, other times dodgy and daunting. For another, it separates you from people who abide beyond your shore. When Charles was young, Penobscots faced a range of dangers when they crossed the river: not only the elemental perils of fast currents, storm surges, thin ice and ice flows, but the proven social risk of being slighted and insulted by white folk on the mainland. This was enough to make one cautious and anxious for security, as it did Charlie. But for some on the reservation, it had the opposite effect, eliciting a kind of recklessness born of the feeling that ultimately, inevitably, the river or the people who lived across it would get the best of you.

The fast-flowing river could be treacherous, but at the same time it had always been a vital lifeline for the Penobscot people who share its name. As a primary food source and travel route, it offered sustenance and mobility – as well as adventure to young and old alike. During his boyhood summers, Charlie used to swim off a ledge on the west side of the island. "One ambition of all the young boys was to get up enough courage to swim across the river," he recalled. "It took courage because of the distance and the swift current. When I was eleven, I finally did it. I swam all the way across – and back. I was really proud."[6] Being cautious did not mean lacking nerve.

By the time he succeeded in this boyhood rite of passage, Charlie had crossed the wide river countless times in the more conventional ways, traveling aboard a canoe or the tribe's hand-rowed ferry bateau in the warmer seasons, trekking atop the ice during the winter and plodding through a sawdust trail spread across the slush of spring. He made the trip much more often than other kids in his generation because his mother had determined that he would receive his primary school education in Old Town rather than at the reservation Catholic mission school run by the Sisters of Mercy. In her opinion, the nuns who taught her older children had focused too much on catechism and not enough on preparing them for higher education. She wanted Charlie to experience a wider world – and apparently knew that with a measure of prodding, this particular son would succeed. "Being the only Indian in a class of forty children was difficult for me," Charles admits. "It weighed on me. I had no connection with them. They used to play during recess while I stood on the sidelines and watched. It took me some time to get acquainted, but I eventually made many friends and became an accepted classmate." He left nothing to chance: "On weekends, I would wash my sweaters and iron my pants so I would look presentable when going to school on Mondays."[7] Fastidious dressing became a lifelong habit.

Ferry bateau service between Indian Island and Old Town on the mainland, c1931. Authors' collection.

In his growing up years on Indian Island, Charlie was only faintly aware that he was part of a remarkable remnant of indigenous people who, almost miraculously, had held on to a sense of who they were despite four centuries of unrelenting pressure imposed by invaders from across the ocean. These interlopers, primarily from the British Isles, had brought diseases, generations of warfare and a stunning series of land grabs that ultimately reduced the Penobscot's vast territory to a tribal reservation consisting of a 60-mile stretch of ancestral river with a string of some 150 small islands located above its major falls. For security reasons, the tribe's main village had been located at the island's southern tip just above the falls. These falls not only offered protection, but also an abundance of fish, speared or netted by Charles' forebears since time out of mind.

Due to disputes about reservation boundaries and hunting and fishing rights, there had always been a certain tension between Indian Islanders and their white neighbors. Like other Penobscot youngsters, Charlie didn't have to be told about this. He saw it in the staring eyes of mainlanders and in the way his own people turned from those stares. This added to his cautious disposition.

But there was another side to Charlie's character, for he landed in a family that generation upon generation showed famously creative daring when facing such tensions. His ancestors include the seventeenth-century grand chief Madockawando, known as much for diplomatic endeavors as for rallying allied warriors against English invaders. This chief's daughter, Pidianeske, married French nobleman Jean Vincent d'Abbadie de St. Castin, a prosperous fur trader and bold military officer who helped Penobscots hold the English at bay. One of their mixed-blood daughters gave birth to Joseph Orono, who became a renowned chief and forged a strategic alliance with the American Revolutionary army headed by General George Washington. On 21 June 1775, Chief Orono offered his tribe's military support in the uprising against British colonial rule in exchange for protection against further encroachment by white settlers threatening Penobscot Indian lands above the head of the tide. Fighting on New England's eastern frontier, the Penobscot and allied neighboring tribes helped white rebels win their independence. Half a dozen Penobscot warriors lost their lives in that freedom struggle, a sacrifice ignored and forgotten by the victorious rebels who quickly resumed repressive tactics of intimidation and dispossession toward their Native allies. As an old man, after a distinguished military career, Charles would remind the Maine State government of his nation's sacrifices under the inspired leadership of his forefather Chief Orono.[8]

One of Charles' great-great grandfathers is John Neptune, son of the famous Penobscot war-chief known as Colonel Orson Neptune. Primarily encamped on Indian Island, John Neptune was a mighty hunter and inspiring orator feared from Nova Scotia to Massachusetts as a shaman-chief with *m'teoulin* (spirit power or magic). His daughter – Charles' great grandmother, Mary Nicola – gained notoriety as a traveling herbal doctress. And her son – Charles' dignified grandfather, Joseph Nicolar – served as Tribal Representative to the Maine State Legislature more often than any other Penobscot to this day and authored the now classic book, *Life and Traditions of the Red Man* (1893). Charles' other grandfather, canoe-builder Sabattis Shay, also served as Tribal Representative.

This line of noteworthy individuals continued through to his parents' generation with his aunt Lucy "Watahwaso" Nicolar and her Kiowa husband Bruce "Chief" Poolaw, who garnered national acclaim as performance artists with a Native rights agenda. His parents, skilled basket makers Leo and Florence Shay, were less showy, but they too were political activists. Beyond Leo's two terms as Tribal Representative to the Maine State Legislature, he and Florence challenged numerous injustices on various fronts – including the fact that Penobscots living on the reservation lacked voting rights, yet all males in the community who were of age were subject to military draft. In sum, Charlie Shay came into this world with a heritage that gave him something to live up to.

Like his ancestors, Charles grew up believing in help beyond the human kind. On his mother's side, he counted *Mándowa'mek* ("Spirit Fish") as a totemic ancestor. Age-old

18

tales relay how this legendary warrior, guided by river-dwelling spirit beings ("water nymphs"), defeated long-feared enemies. Charles did not learn about Mándowa'mek until late in life, yet he often felt and said that "the spirits are guiding."

Charlie "Little Muskrat" with (L-R) his uncle Bruce "Chief" Poolaw, his father Leo Shay, aunt Lucy "Watahwaso" Nicolar Poolaw, Chief Howard Ranco, mother Florence Shay and Roland "Needabeh" Nelson, c1930. Courtesy of Charles N. Shay.

CHAPTER 15
Countdown to D-Day

On 2 April 1944, General Eisenhower left his headquarters at Bushy Park in southwest London to visit the Big Red One encamped at various places in Dorset. He came to inspect, present awards and make a speech. Any illusions that long-running American Indian combat veterans like Melvin Neptune, Howard Anawaush and Anthony Omaha Boy may have had of returning home quickly after the planned invasion were dispelled when Eisenhower declared, "The First Division will be one of the last to go home. If nothing else, I'll just keep you around for good luck."[9]

In the months before D-Day, small teams of American Rangers and British commandos had reconnoitered on the Normandy coast, even scaling its cliffs as they spied out German defenses on dark nights.[10] Meanwhile, training exercises continued apace, with other infantry regiments and Ranger battalions also practicing beach landings at the assault training centers. In late April, for example, troops of the 4th Infantry ("Ivy") Division, which included the cohort of Comanche and other Indians, carried out a large-scale mock invasion of "Utah Beach" at Slapton Sands.[11] Code-named Tiger, this rehearsal near the evacuated coastal village of Strete also included tank battalions, as well as paratroopers of the 82nd and 101st Airborne Divisions. In the predawn hours of 28 April, two flotillas of swift German attack boats[12] on a routine patrol from their French naval base in Cherbourg across the English Channel revealed the harsh reality of what lay ahead when they spotted a secret convoy of American ships crossing Lyme Bay to the Devonshire coast. The convoy included eight LSTs (Landing Ship Tanks) on a practice run carrying combat engineers and delivering jeeps, amphibious trucks and heavy engineering equipment ashore. Seizing the moment, the nine German attack boats successfully torpedoed three of the LSTs. Two sank within minutes, while a third burst into flames but limped back to port. Beyond loss of precious vessels and equipment, this stealth attack claimed the lives of 551 US Army and 198 U.S. Navy men, mostly by drowning. To maintain security and Allied troop morale, all survivors were sworn to secrecy.[13]

The following week, Charlie and his fellow medics participated in the 16th Regiment's final amphibious landing drill on Devonshire's southwest coast, code-named "Fabius." On 3 May, they and the other troops were trucked from Bridport and surrounding villages to their designated marshalling area just outside the hamlet of Martinstown and then taken another 13 kilometers to the port city of Weymouth. There they boarded the attack transport USS *Henrico*, as they had done five weeks earlier for their first amphibious landing and assault training at Slapton Sands.

Early the following morning, the *Henrico* lifted anchor and the final training mission began. Armed with 40 mm anti-aircraft guns as well as two 127 mm deck guns, this year-old transport ship built to hold 1,500 soldiers was equipped with various landing crafts. These included 24 amphibious troop boats, so-called LCVPs (Landing Craft Vehicle Personnel, also known as Higgins boats) that were made of armored plywood and could carry 32 men apiece; three LCPLs (Landing Craft Personnel Large), each with a carrying capacity of 36 soldiers; and four LCMs (Landing Craft Mechanized), 15-meter boats capable of transporting 60 troops or one 30-ton tank. Each landing craft was armed with machine guns and navigated by a coxswain (steersman) with a small crew.

After nearly six hours of travel, the 16th Regimental Combat Team (RCT), including Charlie and other medics, waded ashore on the Torcross end of Slapton Sands beach. Four companies in the 29th Infantry Division's 116th Regiment joined them there, arriving aboard the SS *Empire Javelin*. A sister ship, the SS *Empire Anvil*, carried the 16th Regiment's third Battalion to the beach. More battalions arrived on various other troopships, all fitted out with many small landing crafts capable of transporting groups of 30 or more heavily-armed infantry troops to the shore. To make these exercises as realistic as possible, the military high command ordered the British navy to shell the beach shortly before the assault troops stormed ashore. With live fire immediately in front and directly over their heads, these soldiers would get a sense of the noise and smell of real combat.[14]

For Charlie and others in medical detachments, a sobering part of their training exercises involved litter crews transporting "dead" or "wounded" soldiers to battalion aid stations. From there, casualties were transported to collecting stations and identified by the army serial number embossed on their "dog tags."[15] American soldiers kept two identical aluminum tags around their neck – one on a neck-length chain and one on a short chain attached to the longer chain. When dealing with a deceased soldier, medics removed the tag on the short chain and sent it to the graves registration unit (or hospital) for processing. Then, evacuation squads trucked the ghostly freight to their division's graves registration service clearing station where the deceased's personal belongings were listed and individually bagged.

The importance of this amphibious landing rehearsal could not be overstated. It had been designed to prepare the first waves of assault troops for the daunting task of capturing their designated stretches of a heavily defended enemy-occupied coast, famously code-named "Omaha Beach." For the 16th Regimental Combat Team, the objective was to land on adjoining sectors code-named "Easy Red" and "Fox Green" and capture the two draws or beach exits that led inland to Colleville-sur-Mer and Saint-Laurent-sur-Mer.[16] Simultaneously, the exercise aimed to prime the untested infantry of the 116th Regiment for its task of securing the various draws on the 4-kilometer stretch immediately west of Easy Red, which comprised (from west to east) beach sectors code-named Charlie, Dog (Green, White, & Red) and Easy Green.

Also taking part in this amphibious exercise were American commandos of the 2nd and 5th Ranger Battalions assigned to invade Omaha's westernmost stretches. (Unbeknownst to Charlie, many of these special forces had crossed the Atlantic with him half a year before, and their numbers included Jicarilla Apache, Kiowa, Anishinaabe, Ottawa and Tuscarora warriors.)

Other participants included infantrymen from the remaining combat platoons in the 16th and 116th Regiments, slated to come ashore on the heels of the first assault waves. And preparing to arrive in the wake of the first two waves were the 18th and 115th Regiments, followed by the 26th Regiment which was to land in the late afternoon and then aggressively press inland that evening.[17] Accompanying all these infantry troops were tank battalions, engineer battalions and other military units, including medical detachments. And scattered among these units were an estimated 175 American Indian soldiers, unnoticed in the uniformed masses.[18] No doubt, none of them ever imagined that there were so many in such close proximity.

After returning to Bridport and neighboring towns in coastal Dorset, the regimental combat troops continued their training with long-distance marches, range firing and other intensive exercises, while the medics did what they could to be fully ready to treat and evacuate large numbers of wounded comrades swiftly and efficiently.

Operation Neptune was expected to be a bloody offensive resulting in many thousands of casualties, so medical personnel were preparing for the onslaught, and new army hospitals continued to be constructed all across southern England. Among these was the 186th General Hospital near a new airfield at Fairford, about 160 kilometers north of Bridport. With 158 wooden huts, ten large canvas tents and 1,500 beds, it was ready to handle large numbers of wounded soldiers evacuated from the frontline by boats, ambulances, C-47 transport planes and even airborne gliders. One of the nurses assigned to this U.S. Army hospital was Rose Blue Thunder, a 25-year-old Sicangu Lakota (Brulé Sioux). Born, orphaned and raised on the Rosebud Reservation in South Dakota, she trained as a registered nurse in St. Louis and joined the U.S. Army Nurse Corps in 1943. Beginning in early 1944, 1st Lt. Blue Thunder spent 17 months tending patients at this hospital. As she later recounted: "In England I lived in a tent and worked in the 186th Army tent hospital. You could say this Indian nurse stayed in a teepee."[19]

Among many other American Indian female medical officers stationed in Army hospital units was 1st Lt. Marcella LeBeau, a Lakota of the Two Kettle Band on the Cheyenne River reservation in South Dakota. Once the invasion began, her days and nights would be filled treating casualties at the 76th General Hospital in Herefordshire. During the war, this Army Nurse Corps officer would also serve in France and Belgium. LeBeau's Lakota name is Wigmuke Waste Win – Pretty Rainbow Woman. Her great-grandfather, Chief Joseph Four Bear (Mato Topa), signed the Ft. Laramie Treaty in 1868. Through her grandmother, Louise Bear Face, she was related to Hunkpapa Lakota war chief Rain-in-the-Face, who took part in the 1876 Battle of the Little Big Horn.

As for Charlie, although training kept him busy, it did not consume all his time or attention. While based in

Bridport, he took a liking to Joan, a petite blue-eyed English waitress at a local restaurant. Fresh eggs were difficult to get at the time, but she always made sure "her guy" got some for breakfast. Charlie appreciated the special treatment, as well as Joan's delicate features and feminine form. On occasion, Joan visited her "Indian Romeo" at the infirmary. One evening, while Charlie was there pulling night guard duty, Major Tegtmeyer, commander of the 16th Regiment's Medical Detachment, walked in and discovered that Private Shay was not alone on his army cot. Fully "out of uniform," Charlie decided against standing up to salute his superior and remained under the blankets with "Miss Blondie." Later, Charlie heard from his sergeant Ray Lambert that the major had made note of his romantic dalliance and that he trusted it was understood such adventures would not be tolerated again. Charlie was not punished. The major knew what was ahead and how long the young private would be deprived of such pleasures.

Toward the end of May, infantry troops in the 16th Regiment, along with various attached military units and medics, left Bridport and other Dorset towns and villages nearby. Locals turned out to bid them a warm farewell. One officer described the scene: "As we marched through the village, the people were out waving. Women were crying. Although we hadn't been told, we knew right then that this was it. This wasn't just another practice trip. Those English people are smart. They sense things. How they knew we were on our way I don't know, but they did."[20]

Trucked to the 2nd Battalion's marshalling area near Martinstown, Charlie and other combat medics assigned to frontline platoons were issued gas-impregnated clothing, an assault jacket and a special gas mask. They also had their medical kits fully waterproofed. And last but not least, each soldier was issued three condoms. Infantrymen used one to cover their rifle muzzles to keep them dry. The others were used to protect various small personal items from the seawater.

This did not look like the usual training exercise, but not until 26 May, a day after the camp had been "sealed," did Charlie and his comrades learn that the 16th Regiment had been chosen to spearhead the real assault on Omaha Beach near Colleville-sur-Mer. Meanwhile, their comrades in the Big Red One's other two infantry regiments also left their barracks to be trucked to their respective marshalling areas along the English Channel. About the same time, some 21,000 men of the 4th Infantry Division, including the Signal Company's Comanche code talkers and attached combat units, packed their gear, left their Devonshire quarters and encampments, and trucked to Torquay. There, they boarded the troopships that would take them (and 1,700 vehicles) some 260 kilometers across the Channel to Utah Beach.

The following morning, Charlie and all other assault troops assigned for the invasion of French Normandy remained secluded in their heavily guarded marshalling areas. At about the same time, Pfc. Philip Neptin, a Passamaquoddy combat medic with the Blue and Gray's 115th Regiment, got ready to leave his billet in the historic Cornwall town of Bodmin for an embarkation point near Plymouth. Preparing for action in another corner of England, Passamaquoddy machine gunner SSgt. Walter Meader climbed aboard one of nine heavy bombers in a squadron based in Bassingbourn near Cambridge, north of London. These B-17 Flying Fortresses had just started long-range, daylight missions deep into Germany, targeting the industrial heartland of the Ruhr and other areas. On this sortie, Walter's squadron made a beeline for its dangerous mission to bomb Ludwigshafen – an industrial city situated opposite Mannheim on the Upper Rhine and known for its oil refineries and chemical plants, including IG Farben. They soon ran into serious trouble, later described by the B-17 captain: "Heavy flak and fighter opposition. The air over the target was black with flak bursts when the 91st made its bomb run. One crew member killed and four injured, and aircraft damaged. Sgt. Meader, our waist gunner was killed by a large piece of flak that penetrated his helmet." A veteran of 25 combat missions who held the Distinguished Flying Cross, the Air Medal with three oak clusters, and the Purple Heart, the 20-year-old Maine Indian machine gunner was buried in England at the WWII Cambridge American Cemetery.[21]

On 1 June, the three battalions of the 16th Infantry Regiment were trucked from Martinstown to nearby Weymouth, where the ships that would ferry them across the Channel lay at anchor. Although there had been a minor German air attack on the Weymouth area a few nights earlier, embarkation went according to schedule. Charlie and his comrades in Fox Company once again boarded the *Henrico*, together with troops from the other three companies in the regiment's 2nd Battalion. Meanwhile, 1st Battalion troops boarded the USS *Samuel Chase* and troops from the 3rd Battalion climbed aboard the HMS *Empire Anvil*.

Along with 800 or more other 2nd Battalion GIs crammed into the *Henrico*, Charlie now awaited D-Day H-Hour. Originally, the high command had chosen 4 June for departure, but due to storms the date was set 24 hours later. By then the troops had been four days on board. Finally, with some relief, the convoy left port late in the afternoon of 5 June.

That night, while the moon was out and the sea still rough, Charlie and fellow soldiers on the *Henrico* killed time gambling, shooting dice and playing cards. In the middle of this diversion, something so unlikely happened that for a moment Charlie forgot where he was and where he was going. All he did was glance up inadvertently from the games at hand. And in that moment, he saw him, a fellow

Penobscot from Indian Island walking in his direction. It was Pvt. Melvin Neptune.

Melvin had come aboard the *Henrico* as a scout for his infantry regiment, which was scheduled to land on Omaha Beach a dozen hours after the 16th Regiment. For him, a combat-hardened soldier who had joined the Big Red One four years earlier, an amphibious assault was not new, but this would be his biggest by far. In fact, no one had ever seen an armada of this magnitude, and no one ever would again.

During their unanticipated shipboard reunion, Charlie and Melvin talked about home on the reservation back in Maine, not about the war or the specific battle looming ahead. For Charlie, it was heartening to see a fellow Penobscot who had survived numerous bloody clashes, and Melvin must have relished the relatively recent news Charlie had to offer about Indian Island.

At 10 p.m., Charlie, Melvin and everyone else in the troop hold stopped what they were doing to listen to a brief announcement coming over the intercom: H-Hour for Operation Neptune, the assault on French Normandy's coast, had been set at 6:30 a.m. – less than nine hours from that moment. It was time to bunk down -- to at least seize a chance at sleep, if not sleep itself. The two Penobscots said farewell. Then Melvin vanished as mysteriously as he had arrived. Neither one of them imagined that during the harrowing year ahead, they would rarely be more than 25 kilometers apart yet never catch a reassuring glimpse of one another and the sense of home each represented for the other.

CHAPTER 16

Operation Neptune Begins

Under the cloak of night on the fifth of June, the largest armada the world has ever seen plowed across the English Channel toward France's Normandy shore. It included nearly 7000 ships of every description (from minesweepers to battleships, submarines and landing crafts) loaded with about 134,000 troops. Their charge: Hit five beaches selected as landing sites along an 80-kilometer coastal stretch extending from the Dives River to Cotentin Peninsula.

The same night the armada crossed the Channel, an air fleet of even greater proportion took to the skies in waves and swooped through cloud banks above that not so quiet sea. All told, they numbered over 5,100 bombers, 5,400 fighters and 1,200 Dakotas airlifting more than 18,300 paratroopers.[22] Over 13,000 of the paratroopers were Americans on their way to secure the western flank of the seaborne troops that would storm Utah Beach. The others were British and Canadian forces headed toward the opposite end of Normandy's coast to secure the eastern flank to protect Allied forces landing at Sword Beach and nearby Juno.[23] Some 500 American and Canadian Indians were within this mass of air- and sea-borne soldiers.

Force "O," the initial assault force directed to Omaha Beach, totaled 34,000 men and 3,300 vehicles. This multitude required seven large troop transports, 40 smaller infantry landing ships, 200 landing ships of various sizes for artillery, tanks, bulldozers and other vehicles. For escort duty, gunfire support and artillery bombardment, Force "O" depended on two battleships, three cruisers, 12 destroyers and over 100 other ships. This assault force also comprised 33 mine-sweepers and 585 vessels used in service work.[24]

Charlie's 16th Regimental Combat Team would be the first of three RCTs in the Big Red One to land on Omaha. It alone totaled over 9,800 personnel, 919 vehicles and 48 tanks. Their transport required three large troop ships and more than 60 landing ships of various sizes (for tanks, tankdozers, artillery, trucks and so on), plus five large landing craft for infantry, 18 assault landing craft and 81 LCVPs (Higgins boats). In addition, about 65 amphibious trucks were being shipped across the Channel.[25]

Charlie and fellow Penobscot Melvin Neptune made the crossing on the USS *Henrico* unaware of other American Indians on board. Pvt. Nicholas Naganashe (Odawa) was there, as was Pfc. Nelson Tonegates (Ute), Pfc. N.L. Rackard (Poarch Band of Creek) and Pvt. Alejandro Fragua (Jemez Pueblo). The 16th Regiment's two other transport ships also carried American Indian soldiers, such as Pfc. Nelson Potts of the Prairie Band Potawatomi on the HMS *Empire Anvil*, and Pvt. Ernest Chippewa (Grand Traverse Band of Ottawa & Chippewa) and Pvt. Howard Anawaush (White Earth Anishinaabe) on the USS *Samuel Chase*.[26]

Other ships in the fleet heading to Omaha held a total of up to 170 more American Indian warriors serving in numerous units, including Acoma Pueblo, Apache, Arapahoe, Cahuilla, Cherokee, Chickasaw, Choctaw, Coeur d'Alene, Kiowa, Kumeyaay, Lummi, Maidu, Navajo, Nez Perce, Lakota, Onondaga, Osage, Otoe, Passamaquoddy, Ponca, Salish, Seneca, Shoshone-Paiute, Tuscarora, Wampanoag and Yuchi.

Charlie would disembark in the first wave of the assault, just after dawn. Melvin would come ashore hours later as a scout for his own company in the 26th RCT, which would arrive as part of a large convoy crossing the Channel from Plymouth that afternoon.[27]

Stretched out on his bunk in the troop hold, Charlie tried to get some rest, hampered by the roar of huge turbo-electric engines propelling the fully-loaded attack ship through heavy seas. Deep below deck, as the clock ticked toward 6 June, he could not see or hear the awesome Juggernaut, for he was in its midst.

Just before midnight, an advance squadron of eighteen C-47 Dakotas crossed over the naval armada, flying at low altitude (150 meters) to avoid German radar detection. These planes held the 101st Airborne's pathfinder teams. About half an hour later, 414 Dakotas in several large squadrons flying in "vee-in-vees" formations[28] also roared low above the thousands of ships crowded within a 30-kilometer swath of sea. To protect the C-47s from enemy fighter planes on this dangerous mission, a cohort of Thunderbolts from the 362nd Fighter Group escorted them – with a Menominee Indian piloting one of the bombers.[29] Stealthily cruising toward the Atlantic Ocean, this swarm made a wide bypass around the German-occupied Channel Islands before moving to the Normandy coast. They carried the main body of that division's airborne infantry, about 6,900 Screaming Eagles.[30] Each heavily-packed plane held a "stick" (15 to 18 men). Pvt. Frank Sayers, an Anishinaabe paratrooper known as "Chief," sat in one of the Dakotas. One of his buddies, looking through the windshield and captivated by the moonlit scene below, later described it like this: "There before us, was the invasion fleet, eight and ten ships wide as far as both east and west as I could see…. It was beautiful."[31]

Scheduled to be dropped on the Cotentin Peninsula a half hour past midnight, these Screaming Eagles would jump from very low altitudes into the dark unknown of enemy territory. Their immediate charge was to secure key bridges, major intersections and coastal access routes to support the success of the amphibious landing on Utah Beach. One of the C-47s transported the so-called "filthy thirteen" of a demolition section in the 506th Parachute Infantry Regiment (PIR). Before taking off from Exeter, the men in this stick had applied "war paint" to their faces, shaved their heads like "Mohawks" and been photographed as "Indian warriors" for the *Stars and Stripes*. "War paint" did not provide good camouflage for their nighttime mission to capture and hold or blow up a strategically important bridge over the Douve River, so by now they had probably darkened their faces with oil and brown cocoa like the other paratroopers.[32]

In reconnaissance teams, some paratroopers jumped with two specially-trained carrier pigeons tucked into a vest strapped to their chests. Two different messages had been tied to the legs of each bird. After daybreak, the men would remove one of the missives and release their "flying postmen" to convey the simple truth of their situation: either "We're being wiped out" or "We're winning." [33]

About 6,400 paratroopers of the 82nd "All American" Airborne came in the next wave of 370 Dakotas flying in serial formations 30 minutes behind a small squadron that carried the division's pathfinder teams. Their key objective was to secure a strategic section of the road connecting Cherbourg with Saint-Lô, specifically where it passes through Sainte-Mère-Église 10 kilometers inland from Utah Beach. The 505th PIR had the task of capturing that small town.

One of these Dakotas carried Raymond Brady, a young Cheyenne whose grandfather, Braided Locks, had fought in the northern Plains Indian alliance that defeated the U.S. cavalry in the 1876 Battle of the Little Bighorn. As a pathfinder, Brady formed part of a select team assigned to mark one of the drop zones on the Cotentin Peninsula behind Utah Beach with radio direction finders and luminous panels.[34] Later, he recounted his experience of flying low above the blue-black sea on this unforgettable night:

> I looked down and I could see all kinds of ships, [so close to each other that] I think you could jump from ship to ship. . . . I was one of the first to go in to set-up D-Zones, to set-up a secret instrument to guide the planes carrying other paratroopers. My "stick" jumped first.[35]

In addition to the Anishinaabeg in the 101st and a Cheyenne in the 82nd Airborne, scores of other American Indian paratroopers sat in these planes poised for action: Oglala Lakota and Comanche, as well as Choctaw, Colville, Muckleshoot, Muskogee, Muwekma Ohlone, Navajo, Oneida, Otoe, Odawa, Pawnee, Pima (Akimel O'odham), Potawatomi, Isleta Pueblo, Sisseton Wahpeton, Yanktonai, Yurok, Washoe and Wyandotte.[36]

Like the assault troops in the ships below them, combat-experienced airborne soldiers knew casualty rates were expected to be high and were prepared for the worst.[37] Each paratrooper's netted helmet had an "aid kit tied to the back with its bandages, eight sulfur tablets, and two morphine syrettes, one for the pain and two for eternity."[38]

Within minutes after 2 a.m., all paratroopers had landed – in pastures, marshes, hedges, trees and on barn roofs. They were on schedule, but much went wrong. Due to cloud mass, thick fog and anti-aircraft artillery (flak), most missed their designated drop zones. Numerous men landed so hard that their bones broke, or worse. Some were shot dead while parachuting, a hapless fate shared by a Coeur d'Alene tribesman descended from the legendary shaman-chief Circling Raven. Others drowned in the flooded plains of the Douve or its tributaries, weighed down by about 100 pounds of equipment and hopelessly entangled in cords and nylon canopy.[39] One of them was a 20-year-old Paiute Indian farmhand from the Antelope Valley in eastern California, Pvt. Donald Cornbread of the 508th PIR.[40]

With thousands of men in both airborne divisions severely wounded, dead, captured or simply lost, the pressure on surviving paratroopers became all the greater. For many, firefights with enemy forces erupted immediately. Others remained undetected and had some time to orient themselves. Those who were wounded but still able to fight dosed themselves with morphine and then, like the unharmed, took action. With their weapons (commando knives, grenades and firearms) ready for combat, they moved through the darkness, seeking other survivors with the help of brass clicker-clacker signaling devices known as "crickets."[41] Then they searched for assembly points, formed small fighting groups, identified targets and moved forward to begin battle before daylight.[42] Indian warriors in these advance troops included Sgt. Melvin "Hawkeye" Myers (a Comanche squad leader), 1st Lt. Turner "Chief" Turnbull (a Choctaw who had been severely wounded in Italy) and Pvt. Robert Nez (a Navajo born into the Bitter Water People Clan for the Towering House People Clan).[43]

Meanwhile, shortly before 2 a.m., the *Henrico* reached the rendezvous point for the first-wave ships – an area nicknamed "Piccadilly Circus" after London's crowded traffic junction because so many vessels were slated to pass through there. This space, ten nautical miles wide and situated in the choppy Channel about 15 kilometers north of the Normandy Coast, had just been cleared of acoustic, magnetic and moored mines. And now, minesweepers hastened to clear and mark ten 275-meter-wide passages from there to the beaches – two lanes for each of the beachhead task forces.[44]   The HMC *Sioux* and sister destroyers escorted these vessels to lessen the risk of them being torpedoed by German fast-attack boats prowling in the Channel. American and Canadian Indian sailors served on destroyers, as well as on other vessels in the armada: a Ponca aboard the huge USS *Texas* battleship, a Mohawk seaman crewing on an LST (Landing Ship Tank) and a Coeur d'Alene seaman on the USS *Thompson* destroyer, which had participated in shore bombardment practice at Slapton Sands. Outfitted with four 127 mm guns (five-inch high-explosive shells), as well as four 40 mm and seven 20 mm anti-aircraft guns and five torpedo launchers, she was ready to sink enemy war ships, down aircraft and pulverize bunkers on the bluffs.[45]

Awaiting orders within this huge seaborne assault force, Charlie and the rest of the 2nd Battalion troops half-heartedly ate a breakfast of bologna sandwiches and coffee – welcoming the distraction if not the meal. Then came the command. As Charles recalled soberly, "We were ordered to prepare for debarkation. We went up on deck. It was dark and the seas were rough." Standing among several hundred other men on the crowded deck, Charlie suddenly heard Eisenhower's voice on the intercom. In a pre-recorded speech, also broadcast on the other troopships assembled nearby, the Supreme Allied Commander rallied his men. Too tense to really listen, Charlie caught only bits and pieces:

> Soldiers, Sailors and Airmen. . . . You are about to embark upon the Great Crusade . . . the elimination of Nazi tyranny over the oppressed peoples of Europe. . . . Your enemy. . . will fight savagely. . . . I have full confidence in your courage, devotion to

duty and skill in battle. . . . nothing less than full Victory! Good luck!

At 3:45 a.m. the command came to lower and load the dozen landing crafts that would ferry ashore the first wave of assault troops from the *Henrico*. These LCVPs were just 11 meters long and had ramped bows. Navigated by a coxswain, each jam-packed boat held 30 heavily-armed infantry soldiers, along with a medic and a lieutenant as their commanding officer. Half of these boats were assigned to Fox Company's six assault platoons. The other half, being lowered and loaded on the opposite board of the ship, would carry Easy Company's six platoons. On more ships assembled nearby, first-wave assault troops slated to hit different parts of Omaha and neighboring landing beaches received simultaneous debarkation orders.

To reach the LCVPs, which heaved wildly in the churning sea, infantrymen encumbered by heavy equipment had to climb down swaying cargo nets and then jump. This was no easy task, recalled Charles, who boarded the 3rd Platoon's boat: "It was difficult to load because the sea was rough, and the landing crafts were bouncing. We had to time our jumping into the LC with the rise of the wave."[46] His sergeant Ray Lambert put it like this: "You had to go into the boats just so or your leg would break."[47]

Like other assault platoon medics climbing down into their designated boats, Charlie took his place near the 225-horsepower diesel engine toward the rear, next to the first sergeant (his platoon's second in command) and the demolition team. Just back of them, two Navy crewmen positioned themselves behind the .30 caliber machine guns at the stern, while the coxswain concentrated on the tough challenge of steering their flat-bottomed plywood boat to its designated spot on Omaha Beach – the eastern half of Easy Red.

Up front in the steel-plated bow of Charlie's boat stood his platoon commander, Lt. Gilbert Rollins, followed by five riflemen who would be among the first to hit the beach. Each rifleman had a carbine and 96 rounds of ammunition, and among themselves they carried fragmentation grenades, white phosphorous grenades, a rifle grenade launcher and a bangalore torpedo. Behind them stood four GIs armed with rifles, wire-cutters and two bangalore torpedoes. Then came a soldier equipped with a machine gun plus 900 rounds of ammunition and another with a rocket launcher (bazooka) and 18 missiles, both men assisted by a team member armed with a carbine. And behind them, exactly as they all had practiced, came the platoon's mortar team of four GIs with a 60 mm mortar and 15-20 rounds of ammunition; then two flame-throwers and a crew of five men equipped with several bangalore torpedo poles and pack charges of TNT for blowing up obstacles.

Most of the privates in Fox Company's six platoons were, like Charlie, just 19 or 20 – a few years younger than their sergeants and lieutenants, all of whom were in their twenties. By comparison, Fox Company's 32-year-old commander John Finke was an old man. It fell to him to lead them in their charge of capturing E-3, the wide draw linking the Fox Green area of Omaha Beach to a paved road leading to the east side of Coleville-sur-Mer.

On the other side of the *Henrico*, the six platoons of Easy Company, under command of Captain Ed Wozenski, clambered aboard their LCVPs. Along with Fox Company, they would be the Big Red One's first infantrymen to hit the Easy Red section of Omaha Beach – with Fox Company covering that section's eastern half and Easy Company the western.

Years later Charles recalled this final moment of preparation: "We went to the assembly area to prepare, circling away from the large ships until all the landing crafts were loaded and gathered. Then, about 4 a.m., the order came to proceed to the beach."[48]

It was a relief to pull away from reeking, eye-burning diesel fumes engulfing the LCVP assembly area, but the high seas continued to trouble the troops. Soaked by waves crashing and splashing into their boats, some men feared they'd capsize and drown. Many became seasick and vomited in their helmets or on comrades standing in front of them. Used to rough water and lucky to be in the rear, the Penobscot tribesman felt okay.

Lining up in V formation, Fox Company's coxswains aimed their small boats toward Omaha Beach. Pushed by strong side winds and incoming tidal current, they rammed coastward at eight knots (15 km) per hour. A few hundred meters to Charlie's right, Easy Company's six LCVPs struggled in the same direction. Beyond them, another two dozen landing boats transported Rangers and assault troops of the 29th Division's 116th Regiment to Omaha's western half. And at Charlie's left, barely visible against the pre-dawn skies in the east, twelve more landing crafts lurched through the waves, carrying the 16th Regiment's 3rd Battalion assault troops from the HMS *Empire Anvil.* For a moment, Charlie pictured his fellow medics trying to steady themselves in the sterns of their LCVPs – well-trained young men with whom he had shared meals and jokes for many months.

Standing near the boat's noisy engine and surrounded by the sounds of wind and waves, Charlie did not immediately notice the rumble of bomber squadrons bearing down on German strongholds defending Normandy's beaches. Charged with wrecking enemy defenses for the impending infantry assault, hundreds of B-17 Fortresses, B-24 Liberators, B-26 Marauders and other heavy bombers, escorted by P-38 Lightnings, P-47 Thunderbolts and other fighter planes, had set out from airfields all across southern England to drop thousands of tons of bombs and incendiaries on enemy positions. When low-flying Marauders emerged from the dark grey clouds, hundreds of the small boats rushing toward Normandy came into their view. As later described by a bombardier aboard one of these B-26s, they were "like bunches of ants crawling around down there. . .. I imagined all those young men huddled in the landing craft, doubtless scared to death. I could see what they were heading into and I prayed for all those brave young men."[49]

Dozens of American Indians participated in this air assault – machine gunners, radio men and some pilots. Sergeant John Lee Red Eagle, a young Quapaw machine gunner in the 568th Squadron, flew 6000 meters above the invasion fleet in a B-17. And 19-year-old Ft. Sill Apache Sgt. Inman Gooday hunched in fetal position as a ball turret gunner in a glass bubble protruding from the bowels of another Flying Fortress. Some Indians played a role in the air assault even though they weren't in a plane, such as Pvt. Alexander Ranco, a fellow Penobscot from Charlie's reservation. This 42-year-old bomb-handler had loaded at least one of the B-24 Liberators in the 392nd Bombardment Group now on its way to Omaha.[50]

Just before sunrise, Charlie heard the distant thunder of explosions as the bomber squadrons dropped their deadly loads, lighting up the southern horizon. They continued their barrage for half an hour, bearing down hard in an effort to hammer German defenses, pulverize bunkers and wipe out enemies in their trenches and foxholes on the bluffs.

About 5:30 a.m. Navy war ships a few kilometers behind Charlie's landing craft echoed the onslaught of the fighter planes, aiming heavy 12- and 14-inch guns at the German fortifications on the bluffs. Within the next hour, the USS *Arkansas* and USS *Texas* fired a deafening torrent of artillery rounds over the heads of Charlie and his comrades to destroy any concrete bunkers and artillery batteries that may have survived the aerial bombardment. An hour later, other naval artillery picked up, including from special rocket ships. As an infantry officer coming ashore in a landing craft a few hundred meters to Charlie's right recalled: "Nine thousand rockets, the most beautiful display you ever saw in your life."[51]

In a recent military briefing Captain Finke and other commanders leading the first wave of infantrymen had been assured that a fleet of heavy bombers (each carrying sixteen 500-pound bombs)[52] would carpet bomb the 8-kilometer stretch of Omaha Beach with 100 tons of bombs for every 500 square yards and that a string of German strong points recently built along the Normandy coast and far beyond as part of the Atlantic Wall would be dive-bombed. Of special importance to Finke and his Fox Company troops was the assurance that 186 tons of explosives would be hurled on top of a bunker complex of pillboxes and casemates identified on German maps as WN-62. This was the stronghold guarding the E-3 draw to Colleville and serving as a forward-observer position for a German artillery battery five kilometers inland.

As a young private, Charlie was kept completely ignorant of any such military briefings. Like other enlisted men, he could only focus on his own task at hand. All he knew was that he was ready to do his utmost best to help the men now standing in front of him should they be wounded in this assault. For many, including him, this was their very first day of real combat. Some of their lives would soon be in his hands.

As the small landing boats got closer to the coast, Navy artillery began firing smoke bombs to shroud the infantry's arrival from the enemy. Everything seemed to be going as planned. Then, just as the first assault troops were in position to lower their ramps and charge ashore, a barrage of mortar and machine-gun fire came at them from German strongholds. Unbelievably, their enemies had survived the advance air and sea bombardments, and the smoke screen laid down by the Allies had already been drawn off by the wind.

Worse still, some men noticed debris, then body parts and shattered corpses rolling in the surf – the first victims of faulty military planning and execution.[53] Unfit for navigating these turbulent tidal waters, amphibious Sherman-tanks had sunk to the bottom of the sea well before reaching the beach, and some crew members had drowned. Casualties among combat engineers, who waded ashore just minutes before the infantry platoons, added to the awful scene. These demolition teams, including Lummi, Navajo and Tuscarora tribesmen, had come under devastating mortar fire while detonating mines and blasting 45-meter gaps in the German defenses.

Compounding the horror of seeing so many mutilated, dying and drowning comrades at the outset, Charlie and other 16th Regiment assault troops soon learned that only a handful of the 32 tanks supporting their infantry unit had made it to the beach. Most (in fact, 27) would not be there to assist them when they stormed enemy positions just minutes from now.

As Charlie stood ready to go ashore for his "rendezvous with destiny,"[54] he thought of his beloved mother Florence, whose "prayers guided and protected me. I thought of the Bible, Psalm 23, her favorite:"

The Lord is my shepherd; I shall not want. He leadeth me beside the still waters. . . . Yea, though I walk through the valley of the shadow of death, I will fear no evil, for thou art with me.

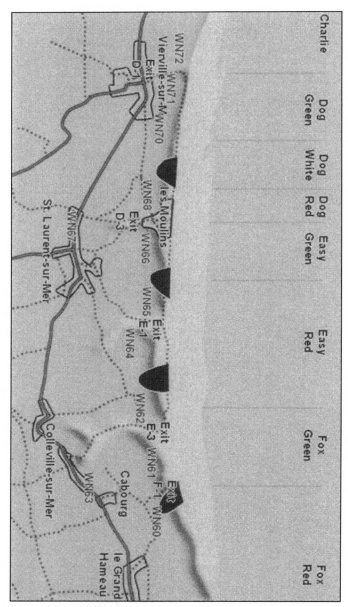

Omaha Beach. Sections where American troops landed and sites of German strongpoints (WNs) that guarded beach exits between high bluffs. On Fox Green, Private Shay and fellow medics provided first aid to comrades shot by enemies entrenched at WN-62. The four American infantry breakthroughs made by noon are marked in black.

CHAPTER 17
Behold the Enemy

Foot soldiers like Charlie would need luck as well as prayers to survive the lethal gauntlet of German defenses along the Normandy seacoast. The expansive tidal flat had been heavily barricaded and thickly mined, and massive firepower strategically positioned to effectively cover the entire coastal sweep. The defenses along this 80-kilometer shore formed a small part of the half-completed 5,300-kilometer Atlantic Wall (*Atlantikwall*), an intermittent chain of protective barriers stretching from northern Norway to the French-Spanish border.[55] Work on this outer wall of what Nazi-German propaganda envisioned as an impregnable fortress had commenced two years earlier.

Construction of Normandy's seacoast defenses had been carried out largely by tens of thousands of French day laborers and foreign forced laborers, including many Russian prisoners of war.[56] Six months before the invasion, German Field Marshal Erwin Rommel had been given command of this colossal rampart. By then, the 52-year-old combat veteran was already legendary as the "Desert Fox," a nickname earned as commander of the Afrika Korps.

With the May 1943 defeat and retreat from North Africa in the wake of Allied amphibious landings fresh in memory, Rommel realized an enemy force must be repulsed at the beach. For early detection of enemy aircraft, he had expanded and improved the giant recently-constructed radar installation near the coast at Douvres-la Délivrande, not far north of Caen.[57] Surveying Normandy's coastal geography, he had called for additional defensive fortifications, including more bombproof artillery emplacements, mortar pits, machine gun nests, slit trenches, fox holes and dug-in sites for *Nebelwerfer* (multi-barrel rocket launchers).[58] Moreover, he had directed a systematic placement of anti-invasion obstacles along the beaches, with especially awe-inspiring impediments along the 8-kilometer stretch extending from Grand Hameau village westward to the town of Vierville-sur-Mer – the beach codenamed Omaha by Allied forces.

It was an impossible obstacle course. Farthest from the shore were magnetic underwater mines set to detonate upon contact. Then, about 250 meters below the high-tide line came a band of "Belgian gates." These 3-meter-high steel-framed structures, strong enough to resist tides, featured vertical girders capable of tearing open a ship's hull. About 30 meters ahead of these gates came a belt of heavy log posts known as "Rommel's asparagus," driven into the sand at an angle, pointing seaward and capped with antitank mines. Some 150 meters below the high-tide mark, the Germans placed a long row of 1.5-meter-high "hedgehogs" made of three crossed steel beams. Next came a line of hundreds of log ramps, some outfitted with anti-personnel and anti-tank mines designed to rip up or overturn enemy landing boats. And last in this line up of deathly deterrents were tetrahedrons, steel-framed pyramids with sharp corners, devised as anti-tank protection.

At the high-tide line on the eastern half of Omaha Beach (from Grand Hameau to Saint-Laurent) stretched a natural barrier: a steep embankment formed by millions of smooth pebbles and small flat stones (gravel) piled up by tide upon tide. Up to 2.5 meters high and as much as 12 meters broad in some areas, this shingle formed an effective obstacle against the passage of jeeps, trucks and other vehicles trying to land. It abutted a level 150-meter sand shelf barricaded with large coils of barbed wire or razor wire and planted with innumerable mines in fields up to 30 meters wide. Signs with skull-and-crossbones punctuated the forbidding scene, announcing, *Achtung Minen*!

Even more fatal hindrance awaited the American soldiers landing at Omaha. With steep bluffs abutting the beach and rising 30-50 meters above sea level, the only way for tanks and other vehicles, even jeeps, to get beyond the beach was via one of the five narrow wooded valleys (draws). To prevent the enemy troops from driving inland, German forces had dug deep anti-tank ditches at the entrance of each of draw. Moreover, they had built fifteen bunker complexes with emplacements for artillery and machine guns known as *Widerstandsnester* ("resistance nests") to further control these inland access routes.

On Omaha's easternmost side, Widerstandsnest 60 (WN-60) defended the draw between the villages of Cabourg and Grand Hameau. And on the other end of this long beach, the Germans constructed WN-74 to secure the westernmost draw leading to the seacoast town of Vierville. These strong points and the ones in between were interconnected by trenches, tunnels and direct telephone lines, all protected by barbed wire and minefields. Among them were WN-61, WN-62 and WN-65, three interlinked bunker complexes guarding the draws to the neighboring coastal towns of Colleville and Saint-Laurent.

Most formidable of all was WN-62, a sprawling complex of bunkers (with concrete pillboxes, casemates, emplacements, tunnels and living quarters layered with cast-iron armor) on the west side of the draw leading to Colleville. Spread over several hectares on elevations ranging from 25-50 meters above the sea,[59] its position was protected by a 300-meter-long anti-tank ditch. Opposite WN-62, some 300 meters across the valley, stood WN-61 guarding the east side of the Colleville draw. And less than 1.5 kilometers inland, at the town's edge, stood WN-63, the local German command post.

Each of WN-62's two fortified casemates, built into the bluffs and featuring steel-bar reinforced concrete walls and roofs some 2-meters thick, was equipped with a 7.65 cm field cannon. The stronghold's arsenal also included two 50 mm anti-tank cannons, two grenade launchers (55 mm mortars), and two water-cooled machine guns in its earthen bunkers, as well as two "twinned" machine guns for anti-aircraft defense[60] and two flamethrowers. Three more machine guns were strategically placed in open positions. All of this stronghold's immense firepower was coordinated with the German soldiers manning the bulwark on the eastern side of the draw.

These fortifications seemed unassailable, but Rommel soon realized that his defensive wall would crumble without sufficient well-trained and highly-motivated fighters. The 716th Coastal Defense Division assigned to guard the 80-kilometer shoreline (that included Omaha) was not invincible by a long shot.[61] Most of its soldiers were 17- and 18-year-olds without combat experience. Organized in 1941 and dispatched to Normandy the following year, this unit was "woefully inadequate…. It was a stretch to even call the 716th a 'German' division, for at least half of it was comprised of non-Germans – Poles, Slavs, and Russians who had been captured on the Eastern Front and who volunteered to serve in Hitler's army rather than be interned in a prisoner-of-war camp. There were even a number of Mongolians from Siberia in Nazi uniform."[62]

Allied intelligence reckoned "that the 716th had only about 800 to 1000 troops with which to man the defenses in the Omaha sector."[63] But they underestimated the Desert Fox, for he had directed the 352nd Motorized Infantry Division to bolster the low-grade and understrength coastal defense division. Troops from both divisions now patrolled and manned this dreadful array of large, medium and small defense posts.[64] Deeper inland, there were many more infantry, artillery and tank battalions, ready to move to the coast and block an enemy attack.

Notwithstanding their huge investment in the Atlantic Wall fortifications, and the recent addition of a combat-experienced division to the coastal defenses between Colleville and Vierville, Germans were caught off guard. On the night of 5 June, Rommel and his colleagues determined there was no immediate threat of an invasion due to the stormy weather. Moreover, Hitler was certain that the assault would be launched across the Strait of Dover, near the French northern seaport of Calais.

Equipped with a telescope, WN-62 served as a 352nd Division artillery observation post connected by radio and telephone to a field battery of four 105 mm howitzers at Houtteville, just over 4 kilometers inland.[65] On the morning of 6 June, a squad of 13 artillery soldiers from that battery and a local platoon of 27 infantrymen from the 716th had taken their posts at WN-62 about 150 meters from the embankment near the shore's high-tide line.

The artillery battery commander at WN-62, 1st lieutenant Bernhard Frerking, stood poised for action at his observation post. Not long after midnight, German soldiers manning the strong points in the Colleville area detected the dull rumble of hundreds of airplanes about 20 kilometers west of them. Soon thereafter, they learned that thousands of enemy paratroopers had landed across the Douve River and engaged in heavy fighting there. Several hours later, between 3:30-4:00 a.m., they sighted vague silhouettes of a handful of mysterious ships some 10 kilometers distant.[66] Then, just as dawn started to break, the haze lifted, and a smoke screen laid down by the Allied fleet slowly vanished.

Private Heinrich Severloh, watching the sea from his machine-gun post at WN-62, was awestruck. Just seventeen days shy of his 21st birthday, he suddenly saw across the entire horizon "an endless, uninterrupted band of ships, some of which were enormous. The sight was eerie, and it was now clear to us that things were about to get ugly. I knelt in my foxhole and prayed quietly…"[67]

Severloh, whose life began on a farm in the Lüneburger Heath,[68] had been drafted into the *Wehrmacht* in the summer of 1942, just weeks after turning 19. Before deployment to the Atlantic Wall in France, he had served as a teamster in a horse-drawn transport unit of an artillery regiment during a brutally-cold winter on the Russian front where he suffered frostbite and became severely ill. After months of hospitalization, he had rejoined his "cursed" old unit soon after its relocation to Normandy. Renamed the 352nd Infantry Division, it had "sustained crippling losses" on Nazi Germany's Eastern Front. Due to health problems, Pvt. Severloh was no longer able to work with the horses and was soon reassigned to the artillery regiment's 1st Battery – the small artillery unit commanded by Lt. Frerking, a 32-year-old former high-school teacher who had been decorated with the Iron Cross for bravery in Russia.[69]

Now on this ominous day, shortly before sunrise, Severloh and his comrades heard the rolling roar of 450 heavy bombers. As if it were a huge swarm of terrifying pterosaurs speeding toward him, Severloh feared his world was coming to an end:

> The noise got louder and louder, and the roar of the motors rose to a hellish thunder as a powerful, ghostly fleet of bombers came directly at us in the grey, cloudy sky. Everyone jumped into the bunkers or shelters; I sought cover in my machine gun pit… Immediately thereafter, their load came howling, whistling and crashing down. The bombs felt like heavy rain…. Everything started to shake, even our small, dug-in observation post vibrated from the detonations, and earth and chunks of limestone fell around close to us.[70]

Franz Gockel, another young private certain he was facing death, crawled under a board that supported his machine gun and shouted, "Hail Mary Mother of God, please save me!" Instead of relief, came a naval bombardment. At about 5:30 a.m., opening up with everything they had, Allied battleships, cruisers and destroyers took aim at the German coastal defenses, shelling relentlessly for about 40 minutes. As Severloh recalled:

> The thunder and crashing of the heavy air attack was hardly over when a thundering, hellish barrage from the sea began.... The ground of the entire line of high coastal bluffs trembled under the head-on attack, and the air vibrated. Thick, yellow, choking dust filled the air. The sky was darkened...it seemed as though the whole world would sink down in a howling and crashing inferno of bursting shells.[71]

For the moment, smoke and dust from the firestorm made it impossible for Severloh to see what was happening at WN-62 beyond his own trench, let alone what might be taking place out at sea. When wind cleared the air, he could not believe his eyes. Despite the enemy's relentless, ear-splitting bombing and shelling, everyone at WN-62 was still alive and their fortifications intact.[72] Unbeknownst to him, one quarter of 13,000 bombs had not been dropped, and planes that had managed to release their high-explosive tonnage had overshot their targets, some by only 20 meters.[73] Most had dropped their payload a few kilometers inland, cratering pastures and killing cows and chickens.[74]

Severloh had hope of suriving this terrifying assault. Secured behind a belt of obstacles, minefields, barbed wire, an anti-tank ditch, yet more mines and fortified concrete, he and his comrades at WN-62 had plenty of ammunition, many thousands of rounds. Most German soldiers were now in place, manning their machine gun nests, mortar pits and other defensive posts. Additional troops were rushing in on bicycles. It would be a miracle if enemies made it through the defense obstacles up to the high-tide line and across the embankment, just 150 meters away.

With the sun about to rise in cloudy skies above the eastern bluffs and all eyes fixed on the dark choppy sea ahead, Severloh stood sentinel in his open machine-gun pit almost 25 meters above the beach:

> At shortly before 0630, after the heavy salvos of the battleships had stopped, I noticed a large, thin and tall boat in our bay, coming from the northeast toward our wide, ebb-tide beach directly in front of our sector, and 600 meters from Strongpoint WN-62. It was a troop landing ship with a shallow hull and a pointed bow, on either side of which large gang planks were lowered. A large number of soldiers appeared at the railing, and began to go down the gangplanks, loaded down with weapons and equipment. One could see it clearly.... They descended the gangplanks calmly, in orderly columns, and jumped into the cold, chest- to shoulder-high water. Many went under for a moment and, half swimming, half wading, they began to move slowly toward the beach in front of our strongpoint. At this time it was almost completely quiet in the bay, and not a shot was being fired. We had strict orders to wait until the G.I.'s were only about 400 meters from the upper beach, and in knee-deep water. [It] was clear to us [they] were about to enter into their own slaughterhouse.[75]

The tall 20-year-old farmer's son aimed his heavy machine gun and waited.

CHAPTER 18
Bloody Omaha

They missed their mark. Not just Charlie's boat, but all six LCVPs carrying Fox Company's assault platoons to the Easy Red sector on the eastern half of Omaha Beach. Two other companies from the 16th Regiment also missed their designated spots on the eastern half. So did most of the landing crafts that were supposed to deliver assault platoons from the Gray & Blue's 116th Infantry Regiment and the 2nd Ranger Battalion to sectors on Omaha's western half. The aim was for all these boats to reach the shore an hour after low tide, 100 meters apart from one another, nearly covering the vast span of the beach.[76] But the strategic plan quickly fell apart, foiled by the stormy oceanic forces of Normandy's coast.

Ferocious tides along Omaha Beach rise and fall as much as seven meters in just a few hours, and the incoming tide generates a strong crosscurrent with an eastward swerve. Mariners unfamiliar with this part of Normandy easily misreckon the current's sidling pressure on their vessels.[77] Briefings and landing rehearsals in southwest England had not sufficiently prepared Navy and Coast Guard coxswains or their commanders for these conditions. That powerful current wreaked havoc on D-Day assault landings.[78]

Fox Company's struggle with the tidal forces reveals how the sea itself became a formidable adversary. When F Company commander Capt. Finke noticed the tidal crosscurrent pulling his boat far from its projected landing on Easy Red's eastern half, he ordered his coxswain to make the necessary correction. But it was too late. Despite changing direction, his boat landed 200 meters east of its objective, where the beach section coded Fox Green abuts Easy Red.[79]

Lt. Aaron Dennstedt in the 1st Assault Platoon's boat immediately to the left of Capt. Finke saw that his boat, too, was way off track. But his coxswain balked at making a correction, determining that "the ground swell was so large that a change of direction was dangerous." That LCVP also missed its mark by 200 meters, beaching just within the eastern edge of Easy Red. Charlie's boat, carrying the 3rd Platoon commanded by Lt. Gilbert Rollins, also came in "a good deal" off target and arrived "directly in front of an enemy strongpoint" (WN-62) on the western edge of Fox Green, near Capt. Finke's Headquarters Detachment boat. [80]

The boats carrying Fox Company's three other platoons fared even worse. The 2nd Platoon's landing craft just to Charlie's right carried his friend and fellow medic Pvt. Edward Morozewicz, with Lt. Bernard Rush in command. Realizing they were being pulled from their aim, Rush shouted to his coxswain to bear west to counter the eastward current, but the Navy seaman resisted until it was too late. As a result, he landed toward the center of Fox Green, 800 meters east of his assigned spot on Easy Red.[81]

The 4th Platoon, under Lt. Glendon Seifert, motored about 100 meters left of Charlie's boat and had troubles early on. It was separated from the rest of F Company when a Landing Ship Tank (LST – a much larger and faster boat transporting two Sherman tanks and a bulldozer) cut through F Company's V formation.[82] After catching up with the other platoons, Seifert thought they were back on course, but his boat's coxswain disputed that. A hundred meters from shore, he "turned the boat around, returned 300 meters, then came back to the beach about 1,100 [meters east] of the proper position."

The 5th Platoon, led by Lt. Otto Clemens, also landed at Fox Green hundreds of meters east of its slated location.

Its navigator's hand was forced by tide and enemy fire: "As this boat was approaching the shore, it seemed to be bearing too far to the [west]. An artillery shell landed to the right of the boat. The coxswain swung [east] because of this burst but a shell then lit to the [east] of the boat. Lt. Clemens said, 'Take her in. Let's get the hell off this ship.'"[83]

In sum, among Fox Company's six assault platoons scheduled to beach on Easy Red, only one platoon did so. The rest ended up at Fox Green. This is also where many other assault platoons in the first wave were mistakenly dropped, including five of Easy Company's six landing boats. Radically missing their designated destinations on Easy Red's western half, they intermingled with three of F Company's boats in the center and eastern half of Fox Green near the Coleville draw. When E Company's commander realized that all but one of his platoons had come ashore some 2 kilometers east of their scheduled landing point, he burst out: "How anyone briefed could have made such an error, I will never know."[84]

An even-greater botch doomed four platoons of the 29th Infantry Division's 116th Company, which were dropped some 3 kilometers east of their intended position on the western half of Omaha Beach. Completely off target, they landed on top of the 16th Regiment's assault platoons at Fox Green, adding chaos to chaos.

Coming in at low tide, about 50 minutes past sunrise, the first LCVPs ran aground on sand bars some 200 meters offshore. It was 6:40 a.m. They were ten minutes late. When the coxswains yelled, "This is it!", brave men led by young lieutenants kicked down the bow ramps and steeled themselves to storm the beach. Many had been seasick and were anxious to get off their boats. Others, paralyzed by fear, were shoved forward brusquely. Some, after hours of standing packed together, were so cramped they could hardly move their legs. The troops had been instructed to jump and spread out immediately in a V formation about 30 meters across. Little came of that, for as they plunged into the cold sea, many were instantly strafed by machine guns and pounded by exploding mortar shells.

The strafing came from German machine gunners in fortified concrete bunkers, trenches and foxholes strategically situated on the high bluffs – a network of enemy fortifications pitifully undamaged by the Allies' intensive bombing and shelling raids from air and sea. German rocket launchers also assaulted the American invaders, discharging high-explosive fragmentation shells and incendiary projectiles that set men aflame with burning petroleum. Those on fire hurled themselves overboard in desperation. An avenging god of death could not have chosen a more lethal location than Fox Green in front of E-3, code name for the entrance to the vallée du ruisseau des Moulins ("Mill Creek valley"), which was strategically covered by intensive German cross-fire from the twin strongpoints WN-61 and WN-62.

When the infantrymen in Charlie's platoon leapt from their landing craft, they found themselves in water 1.2-1.8 meters deep (sometimes more due to deep runnels), with an undercurrent that carried them farther east. All struggled to find some footing, and many drowned, unable to swim or pulled down by heavy equipment.[85] As a medic, Charlie was among the last to jump from his boat as it rocked and rolled in the sea. Six decades later, this is what he recalled:

> The minute the ramp went down, we were under murderous fire – machine gun, artillery and mortar. Even before the ramps went down, all hell had broken loose on the ships. Some LCVPs took hits with a full load. The sweeping action of German gunfire hit some men as soon as the ramps dropped, and they went down in the water dead. Or they were wounded and then drowned. Once the ramps

were down it was every man for himself. When I left the ramp, I landed in water up to my waist. Some landed in water up to their chests. Each of us was loaded down with all sorts of gear. I was carrying two medical bags.[86]

Charlie was lightly packed compared to soldiers armed with rifles and hauling heavy equipment such as mortars, bazookas, torpedoes, 72-pound flamethrowers, ammunition belts and bags with rockets, explosives and so on. Nonetheless, it was a mighty struggle for him to push forward against surf and fire. Stumbling into a deep runnel, he found himself in chin-high water and fought the downward pull of his water-logged uniform and gear. Having grown up on the bank of the Penobscot River, the medic known back home as Little Muskrat started to swim. The rough sea was an enemy nearly as daunting as the Germans. Yet, for all its perils, water offered a slight possibility of protection for those who could swim. As Charlie's staff sergeant Ray Lambert later recalled: "We learned the best chance to live and reach the shore was to go as far under water as you could."[87]

To avoid drowning and to make any headway, many soldiers had no choice but to abandon the bulky equipment that weighed them down, and sometimes even their rifles. Surrounded by exploding mines and relentless German firepower, with nothing but survival on his mind, Charlie made it across a wide runnel to shallower water. Finding ground underfoot, he slogged his way to one of the anti-invasion obstacles that Germans had erected on the tidal flat – the first of several that would provide minimal momentary cover in his scramble up the beach. The Indian medic recalled his ordeal like this: "We tried to get to the beach and find some protection from the murderous fire coming at us. We used the steel and cement triangles that blocked ships as we moved through the water."[88] Pausing briefly, Charlie tried to catch his breath, but it only seemed to quicken as he noticed men being gunned down, pierced by shrapnel, blown to pieces by mined obstacles or picked off by sharpshooters.

Pvt. William Funkhouser, a mortar gunner in Charlie's platoon, described what he experienced when he jumped from their boat into the water:

> [It was] not quite waist deep and I thought, "Maybe I won't get wet all over." Of course, we started going in and the water got deeper. . . . It seemed like forever before we got through the deep channel and up the other side, and I got to the edge of the water [when] to my left front was this white explosion. There wasn't any concussion to it. Some of the men carried TNT to blow the pillboxes. A [22-year-old] guy named Speckler . . . was carrying this TNT and what set it off no one ever knows. As far as ten feet were body parts. The biggest was as big as my fist and just white as snow. I was just fascinated as I looked at that. I thought "I can't crawl through that." I was going to jump up and run. [I] stood up and my legs wouldn't hold me and down I went. If I never moved from there, that didn't bother me, thinking I was hit in the legs. You can't imagine how scared I was. Anyway, I chucked my 60 mm mortar, shut my eyes and I crawled.[89]

From behind an obstacle, Charlie could see nearby to his right Fox Company's commander Capt. Finke and executive officer Lt. Howard Pearre, along with 28 soldiers of the Headquarters section, pressing toward the tidal flat. The men following Finke had "hit the water with only rifle fire around them,"[90] and for the moment, their platoon was intact. Soon, they became mixed in with many soldiers from Charlie's platoon, all striving toward the beach. "Before all reached the water's edge, however, mortar shells started landing in the water" and felled several of Finke's men. Among the wounded and killed was 33-year-old Lt. Pearre, who died on the spot. This valiant career soldier had fought in North Africa and Sicily where he had been wounded and awarded a Silver Star.

With Finke's lieutenant dead, Sgt. Thaddeus ("Thad") Lombarski stepped in as platoon leader directly under the captain's command. Straining forward through chest- or even neck-high water, some of his exhausted and wounded men drowned. Those who pressed on bumped against mutilated bodies rolling in the surf. Reaching the advancing waterline of the rising tide, Finke's gunners hustled to set up light machine guns for cover against fire from the WN-62 pill box positioned on the bluff. But as they worked, an "enemy machine gun raked the water's edge and all the men hit the dirt in a fully exposed position." Two squad sergeants took a hit, and Finke's machine gunner was mortally wounded.[91]

Like Charlie, most Fox Company soldiers managing to make headway sought cover behind iron hedgehogs and other defense obstacles. Spurring on troops within earshot, "Capt. Finke yelled to the men to move forward, and in little groups they advanced to the high water line."[92] There they could find slightly better short-term shelter behind the impressive natural barrier of gravel and pebbles built up by the tide over centuries. For men desperate for even a modicum of protection, that long, high shingle was a gift from the sea. But it took guts to get there. Immobilized by fear, many refreshment troops not yet battlefield tested remained hunkered down behind the obstacles. Even many soldiers who had proved their bravery in heavy combat previously were too shocked to move, stunned senseless by the magnitude of firepower unleashed upon them – and by the sight of bombs, mortars and iron-hot shrapnel ripping open bodies and severing arms, legs, even heads. Lifeless men or parts of them bobbed in the incoming tide, colliding with the living. Charles would never be able to forget – or talk about – these gruesome sights, sounds and smells. Confronted with more horror than he could bear to describe, he would simply recall "The water was red with blood."[93] Capt. Finke described the harrowing situation:

> We had a great deal of difficulty getting the men to move. There was a great deal of enemy fire and they would take cover behind some of these obstacles that were there to catch assault craft. They were about the size of [a] ten or twelve foot pole with a teller mine on the top of it. The whole area was just full of these poles. Well, [they] didn't provide any [real] cover so you just had to force [the men] to move no matter how you did it. It so happened, I had sprained my ankle in the marshalling area and had to go ashore carrying a cane instead of a rifle. I used it to very good effect to just whack people until they moved. It was very rough getting up the beach because the sand was wet and deep, and people would sink in…. We couldn't run. With packs that ranged from 30 to 100 pounds, and all of our clothes and equipment waterlogged making it much heavier, we at least couldn't do much running.[94]

Recalling how he dealt with his own fear, Finke said he overcame it by focusing all his energy on getting his men to move as quickly as possible to the shingle for a measure of cover against the machine guns and rifle fire coming from the bluffs: "You're thinking about what you have to do and more or less forget about your own personal danger because you don't have time to think about it."[95]

Crouched behind the cross-beams of a hedgehog at the water's edge, it became clear to Charlie that he would have to cross about 200 meters of tidal flat to reach the shingle. Seeing carnage all around him, he got up to make a run for it, expecting to sprint. Instead, he staggered forward, hindered by soft ground and his soaked, sand-filled uniform. Somehow, he succeeded. In his words, "It was complete chaos. I don't know how I made it to the beach."[96]

An officer coming ashore a few dozen meters to Charlie's right, later described what they and so many others experienced during the longest run of their lives:

> You're terrified, as anyone would be. And every time I got up I thought that it was pure terror that was making my knees buckle until I . . . realized I had about 100 pounds of sand in those pockets that had accumulated on top of the maybe 50 or 60 pounds that we were all carrying in. So it wasn't just pure terror that was making our knees buckle. Our pockets were full of sand.[97]

Meanwhile, some 250 meters west of Charlie's cohort, Lt. Aaron Dennstedt led the charge of his Fox Company platoon. This 24-year-old officer, a former University of California student from North Dakota, had fought in Africa and received a Silver Star in Sicily. His unit had taken fire as their boat ramp came down, and some of the men were hit as they jumped into neck-deep water. Undeterred, Dennstedt led the way forward and reached the tidal flat. Eying the high-water mark with its protective shingle only 75 meters from his position, he stood, turned toward the sea and yelled to his troops to "keep moving. At this moment he was killed by enemy machine gun fire." [98] Soon, the incoming sea covered him, and the strong undercurrent pulled his body into the deep – as it did the bodies of so many soldiers who were severely wounded or instantly killed.

Those not yet killed or mortally wounded still had to cross all those meters to the shingle. "Of the 30 men and 1 officer leaving [Dennstedt's] boat, only 14 reached this cover." Similarly, by the time Capt. Finke and the Headquarters unit got there, only 17 of the men from his boat were present. Of these, just ten had escaped being wounded and were fit to fight. As for Charlie's platoon, "about twenty reached the cover, half of them wounded."[99]

Some 250 meters east of where Charlie's boat landed, Fox Company's 5th Platoon, led by Lt. Otto Clemens, was struggling toward the shore directly in front of the E-3 draw. Clemens, an exceptional 21-year-old officer from Wisconsin, had been awarded the Distinguished Service Cross for heroism in Sicily. His unit had a lucky start because they had difficulty lowering their boat ramp, and at the moment it finally opened the German "machine gunner was out of ammunition or changing his barrel. Most of the men got off the boat in good shape before the gun[ner] again opened up."[100] But their luck was short-lived. After entering waist-deep water that extended about 50 meters, "they were subjected to machine gun and rifle fire so that many were wounded. [The] fire was intense but as the group moved forward everyone kept yelling 'Keep moving, Keep moving.'"

While waving at his soldiers and urging them to hurry on, Clemens took a hit and died at the edge of the tidal flat. Just seven of the 31 men in his unit reached the shingle. "One of these was wounded. A few others crawled along very slowly just ahead of the tide." Their medic, Charlie's brave-hearted Jewish friend Pvt. Morris Levine, managed to give first aid to his comrades even though he himself had been seriously wounded.[101]

Meanwhile, some 600 meters beyond the spot where Otto Clemens took his last gasp, Charlie's friend Pvt. Edward Morozewicz had just jumped into the cold water.

His unit, led by Lt. Rush, fared slightly better than Fox Company's other assault platoons. Their boat "beached about twenty or thirty meters from the land [where] the water was so shallow that the men could move quickly."[102] Following comrades, the young medic from New Jersey waded toward the tidal flat. "Between the boat and shore there was small arms fire, but no one seemed to go down in the water. On the beach the [automatic riflemen] fanned to the right and left, firing right from the edge of the water. The men generally started running across the beach. At this point it is about a hundred meters to the [shingle at the] high water line. Both [automatic rifle] gunners were hit almost immediately." One died instantly. The other, who "lost his right leg from a shell fragment," would probably have preferred that fate. Despite his severed leg, "he pulled himself a hundred meters to the [shingle]. He died several hours later as the proper aid could not be given him." Just twenty of the soldiers in Morozewicz's unit made it to the shingle, and "about half of these were wounded," as was their platoon commander.

Coming in at 6:50 a.m., ten minutes later than the rest of Fox Company, the assault platoon commanded by Lt. Seifert landed about 1,100 meters east of their designated spot. There they "jumped into breast-deep water. Small arms and mortar fire fell all around but the men cleared the water well."[103] Hurrying across the tidal flat, the platoon commander and three soldiers were wounded, but reached the shingle along with all other men in their unit. Tragically, that embankment offered little solace for the 31-year-old lieutenant. As one of his sergeants later recalled: "I came upon Lt. Seifert, flat on his back, just staring blankly, shot through the throat, just below the Adam's apple. His chest was covered with blood, which was continuing to pump slowly from the wound."[104] Not long afterwards, this unfortunate officer from Philadelphia died of his wounds.

All told, between their landing points and the shingle, Fox Company had already lost nearly a quarter of its men, and all but two of its officers were killed or wounded. As Capt. Finke recalled, "I might have lost 25 percent of my command before we even got to the [embankment]. Of the four officers that were killed on the beach from my company, I think three of them were killed almost right at the water's edge."[105]

Hunkered behind a stretch of shingle that extended eastward some 1,100 meters from the eastern end of Easy Red and all across Fox Green, F Company's widely scattered survivors found themselves mixed up with the assault troops of Easy Company, their regiment's sister unit in the 2nd Battalion, and also soldiers from the 29th Division who had landed far amiss from their target on western Omaha. With many of their sergeants among the casualties, most were left leaderless. Describing the confusion, Charles said,

> We were expected to land and operate as units, but the units couldn't function as they should have because men were separated from their units and so many leaders had been hit. . ... It was only thanks to the courage of officers on down to privates who stepped forward to motivate GIs to get off their butts that our advance continued. . . . If they hadn't taken initiative to coordinate, I don't know what would have happened. I remember Captain Finke on shore. He was one of the officers able to organize people.[106]

With so many casualties among the lieutenants, surviving sergeants in assault platoons assumed leadership over troops still alive and able to fight. Behind the tenuous shelter of the shingle, Charlie and his fellow soldiers tried to regain courage and gather their wits. Although this high pebble-and-gravel bar offered some security against incoming bullets, anyone who raised his head for a quick glance, or accidentally exposed a body part, was likely to pay a price in blood. Sharp-eyed snipers firing from the bluffs tried picking them off one by one. Moreover, at any moment a mortar shell or some other lethal device could explode above them and hurl a hail of shrapnel or burning petroleum – perhaps even poison gas, so they feared. Describing the precarious position of soldiers huddled up against the protective barrier at the high-tide line, one sergeant recalled:

> Most of the time that we were behind the shingles we kept our faces buried in the side of the bank. Shingles are small stones that resemble river rock and had been built-up like a roadbed. They were smooth and mostly flat, just right for skipping across a stream back home. But these stones burst like grenades when hit by a bullet and we had to keep our faces protected from the rock fragments.[107]

Peril behind the barrier paled compared to the deathtrap on the other side. Now serving directly under Fox Company's captain, Sgt. Lombarski ordered his platoon's wireman to "blow the barbed wire" just beyond the shingle. This extremely dangerous task required "crawling thirty meters exposed to small arms and mortar fire."[108] Although carbines were useless from this distance, men who had not dropped or lost their weapons readied them, removing the condoms they'd placed over the muzzles to keep them dry. Meanwhile, one of the squad leaders set up his light machine gun to fire on the pill box in front of them, only to be shot dead seconds later. Two other gunners were wounded.

Capt. Finke realized that any advance up the bluff or into the E-3 draw would be suicide, for an attacker attempting to storm forward would be dead within seconds, given the arsenal of guns firing from WN-62's position about 150 meters in front of his men. If miraculously missed by a bullet, they would likely be blown up by one of hundreds of mines buried in the long stretch of beach sand ahead. A fellow commander summarized the impossible challenge presented to Finke and his men stuck in front of this terrorizing strongpoint: "To cross 400 yards of low water beach and climb a formidable bluff to the enemy's main defenses was little short of murder."[109]

Paralyzed by this grim situation, Capt. Finke and the fraction of Fox Company soldiers with him would be pinned down for more than four hours. During that time, the tide would rise quickly and claim the lives of soldiers too seriously wounded to escape its flow. Successive waves of assault troops would come ashore, many also missing their scheduled landing points and losing enough men to doom the mission. Portable radios, damaged by seawater, would be found useless, forcing those in command to rely on runners whose odds for success were minimal.

Meanwhile, first-wave infantrymen in the two assault companies of the 16th Regiment's 3rd Battalion slated to land on Fox Green in the first wave also wrestled the tide to get there. As L Company approached Omaha, one of its landing boats sank in the heavy sea and another was hit by artillery. Those that reached the shore came in 30 minutes late and landed on Fox Red, hundreds of meters east of their designated spots. There, on Omaha's narrow, easternmost sector, they found themselves facing German strongpoint WN-60. This bunker complex guarded a minor draw to the small seacoast villages of Cabourg and Le Grand Hameau and was less formidable than strongpoints defending the other four inland draws. Nonetheless L Company suffered 63 casualties that morning.

The six landing boats of its sister unit in the battalion, I Company, also veered off course, but ultimately managed to land at Fox Green, albeit ninety minutes late. They found themselves among scattered remnants of over a dozen other infantry platoons. The 3rd Battalion's other two companies fared a bit better, landing on the eastern half of Fox Green 35 minutes behind schedule. Scores of soldiers and several officers in these units were also wounded or killed on the beach. But there were determined survivors, such as rifleman Pfc. Nelson (*Me-Nom-Ni*) Potts, a Prairie Band Potawatomi from Kansas, who went on to distinguish himself for "heroic achievement" that deadly day.

Similar chaos and carnage ensued during landings all across Omaha, especially on the beach's westernmost end. There, near the Vierville draw, code-named D-1, the 116th Infantry Regiment's Alpha Company came ashore under withering machine-gun fire from two German strongpoints.[110] In just ten minutes from the moment this assault unit began disembarking at 6:36 a.m., all its officers became casualties. And before reaching the shelter of the seawall, every sergeant was either killed or wounded. Moreover, firepower also ravaged the adjoining medical team boat, hitting every man in that section. Soldiers still capable of wading pushed some of their injured comrades ashore, perhaps inadvertently turning them into living shields. A Cherokee radio man from Bedford, Virginia, was among those killed.[111] Leaderless and virtually without weapons, Alpha Company "had lost 96% of its effective strength."[112]

Already, two things had become terribly obvious: The enemy's numbers, arsenal and combat experience vastly exceeded what the Big Red One had been told to expect, and far too many young men were paying the ultimate price due to tragic miscalculations and tactical errors. Within just one horrific hour, Omaha Beach had already become an American graveyard.

CHAPTER 19
Medic! Medic, Help!

As a combat medic attached to one of Fox Company's six assault platoons, Charlie was an unarmed "first-aid man" simply identified by a red cross stitched onto a white cotton band tied around his upper left arm. Like others wearing that *brassard*, he repeatedly risked his own life so that injured men might live another day. On D-day morning, all along the 8-kilometer stretch of Omaha Beach, he and many dozens of other medics tried desperately to save lives. Universally praised by combat veterans as "the bravest of the brave," they did their job under withering enemy fire.[113] Among combat medics on Omaha, "heroism was the only standard procedure."[114]

Catching his breath behind the shingle on the beach's Fox Green sector near the eastern edge of Easy Red, Charlie knew that he and all the men near him were "directly in front of an enemy strong point [with] several emplacements and pill boxes about two hundred yards away."[115] He also knew that the gravel-and-pebble barrier offered no guarantees against mortar shells or sharpshooters. In his words, "The Germans had their bunkers and trenches and were looking down on us. We were sitting ducks."[116] There was proof of this, for sniper fire hit six soldiers behind the shingle in his vicinity.[117] Many others arrived there already wounded. According to a 16th Infantry Regiment report, "As far as the eye could see, bodies were packed behind this ledge – men who were moaning with pain, and those who would moan no more."[118]

Within seconds of reaching the shelter of the shingle, Charlie began what he had prepared for but never experienced – tending to comrades gashed by shrapnel, pierced by bullets or butchered by bombs. Some were missing body parts, all were exhausted by agonizing pain. Screams were drowned out by ear-splitting explosions. Only a mysterious divine power could save the severely wounded from almost certain death. Not giving any thought to metaphysics, Charlie focused on the challenging task at hand:

> I sought the protection of the embankment to recover my senses and recover from the shock. It took a few seconds. Then I began performing the duties I'd been trained to do – applying bandages and sulfur on large wounds, giving morphine in cases of serious pain and making the men as comfortable as possible. Each infantry man had his own waterproof-covered bandages attached to their belt, so if I didn't have enough I used those.... We had tourniquets for serious bleeding, but they're dangerous because they need to be released every 4-5 minutes. I instructed those who were lucid to loosen and then retighten their tourniquets and then I moved on to the next man. I wasn't able to go back to them. I couldn't focus on individuals.... There was a continuous unloading of troops so the number of wounded kept growing.

Charlie's description of the mounting number of fellow soldiers amassing behind the shingle during the morning hours echoes that of every other report of the scene, including this one from his regiment's medical detachment commander:

> As far as eyes could see in either direction [the] huddled bodies of men; living, wounded and dead, as tightly packed together as a layer of cigars in a box. Some were frantically, but ineffectually, attempting to dig into the shale shelf [shingle], a few were raising themselves above the parapet-like edge and firing toward the concrete protected enemy [in bunkers] below the [tops of the] bluffs, as well as those on the cliff above, but the majority merely huddled together face downward.[119]

Like scores of other medics who survived the landing, Charlie "worked up and down the shingle pile, bandaging, splinting, giving morphine. . .."[120] As described by a staff officer, first-aid men were "the most active members of the group that huddled against the seawall. With the limited . . . facilities available to them, they did not hesitate to treat the most severe casualties. Gaping head and belly wounds were bandaged with the same rapid efficiency that was dealt to the more minor wounds."[121]

In this frenzy, time vanished quickly – as did the tidal flat between sea and shingle. Regardless of human suffering, the tide was rising as it always does. Looking up from his gruesome job, Charlie noticed maimed bodies tumbling in the surf, rolling in his direction. Searching for easy targets, enemy sharpshooters also spotted the injured and systemically picked them off. Pvt. Waldo Werft, one of the medics in Charlie's regiment, recalled them being targeted "like fish in a barrel."[122]

Their helpless plight seized Charlie's attention. Fully exposed to enemy fire, he rushed back across the open tidal flat toward the water line:

After treating all the GIs in my area, I glanced back where I'd come from. I saw many men floating in the sea face down, drowned. Others were wounded, weighted down. . . . The tide was coming in and they couldn't help themselves. Once I saw so many wounded in the water who couldn't make it, I went back to the water. . . . My first thought was that they were going to drown, and I needed to help them. I was able to help many by pulling them out of the water to the shore line. They had important gear – bangalore torpedoes, machine guns. I dragged as many as I could up to the embankment – until I was exhausted. Then I paused and began again until I couldn't do more. I don't know where my strength came from. Those I helped could have been from any platoon. I wasn't interested in who anyone was, or which platoon they came from. I have no idea how many I pulled to safety or how many I saved.[123]

One of the soldiers from Charlie's landing boat, Pvt. William Funkhouser, well remembered seeing the Indian medic pull "a big guy about twice his size" from the water's edge.[124] And Funkhouser, like so many other soldiers, also dragged a drowning comrade from the waves.

Charlie's friends, Fox Company assault platoon medics Edward Morozewicz and Morris Levine, also conducted themselves heroically on Omaha that morning. So did James Stickles ("Sticks"), another friend who had trained with them. Sticks landed just west of Charlie around 7 a.m. in the second wave of assault troops.[125] Assigned to the 2nd Battalion's G Company, he worked "away from the cover of the shingle, patching up men" on Easy Red. And, like Charlie and other medics, he also went up and down the beach, pulling injured men from the incoming tide, dragging them to the shingle and treating them as best as he could.

Treatment "wasn't much more than applying tourniquets, giving wounds a quick cleaning, applying sulfa and/or the new wonder drug Penicillin (the US pharmaceutical industry had produced a record-breaking 100 million units of penicillin the previous month), giving a shot of morphine and waiting for an opportunity to take the man by litter down to a landing craft that was going back to the mother ship for another load [of troops]."[126]

Charlie was not the only American Indian medic tending injured soldiers on the beach. Among others on hand were Pvt. Howard Anawaush (a 23-year-old White Earth Anishinaabe from Minnesota)[127] and Cpl. Calvin Daily (a 19-year-old Otoe-Missouria tribesman from Red Rock, Oklahoma). Daily had crossed the sea that night aboard the SS *Empire Javelin* and landed with a 116th Regiment assault platoon somewhere on the beach. Passamaquoddy medic Pfc. Philip Neptin from Sipayik in coastal Maine came ashore a few hours after Charlie with the 29th Division's 115th Regiment.[128] And somewhere on the western half of the beach, Kiowa combat medic, Pfc. Truman "Kaw-al-baw" Anquoe, offered first aid to wounded Rangers with whom he had trained in Wales and come ashore in the second wave that morning. Born "in a teepee" in the Great Plains, this tribesman from western Oklahoma had entered the army in 1942:

> I could have got in infantry, but I told them I didn't believe in killing, so I got in medical corps. But even when I was in service, I still turned to my tribal ways to guide me and direct me and to help me through the bad parts of life. . . . When we went to the shore we could see the bombing of beaches with shells, and I hit the ground. The guy by me, I was supposed to tag him killed in action or wounded in action, I'm supposed to tag him, so they could identify him, notify their relatives through that, so I

tagged this man, this boy. He was a northern Indian, he was from Wisconsin I think; I forgot his name but the first person who landed . . . was American Indian on D-day. So I stayed with him for a while; I thought about his parents, about his loved ones. In my heart I prayed for him, and I still remember his face today. There was thousands of men killed to secure that beach, American soldiers. And we were sent in on the second wave to look for the wounded and to treat them, and if they're in pain we'd give them a shot of morphine, and we had a collection station where we collected all these wounded men. Then the Navy came in with boats, LCI's, we would load them on, these wounded guys, and there were hundreds of them on these landing crafts that took them to a hospital ship. And that was the most gruesome thing I've ever saw in my life. There were land mines, barbed wire, personnel mines, anti-tank mines, that when you touched one that tripped it, exploded. [But] what I saw was unbelievable, the dead American soldiers, the wounded. When they got wounded, the first thing they turned to was God.[129]

Litter bearers for the wounded in Charlie's regiment were in short supply on eastern Omaha for much of the morning. One major reason was that German artillery hit the large LCI transporting the 16th Infantry Regiment's entire collecting company as it tried to land on the Fox Green sector of the beach at 8:30 a.m. Fire broke out and men tried to escape from the smoking hold, only to be raked by machine guns from WN-62 and other positions on the high bluff. Fifty-six medics – including many litter bearers – were wounded or dead. In the mayhem, several men made it to the beach, but when the ship's ramp was shot away, resulting in more casualties, the LCI backed away.[130] Withdrawing from that deadly stretch of beach, the "floating fuel tank" (as one medic denigrated this 25-meter-long landing craft) then maneuvered a few hundred meters to the right, and the men started debarking at Easy Red. Again, a number of medics were wounded by enemy fire "as they were coming off the ship. During this time other direct [artillery] hits went into the holds," setting three of them on fire and causing panic among the survivors. With the ship "listing badly to starboard and . . . rapidly sinking," crew members managed to extinguish the fire and maneuver the LCI back to the *Samuel Chase* – with the dead and wounded on board.[131] Also on board were many of the litter bearers needed to evacuate the wounded from the beach. According to Maj. Tegtmeyer, the 35-year-old surgeon who commanded the 16th Regiment's Medical Detachment, "early evacuation would have saved half of our losses."[132]

Maj. Tegtmeyer had come ashore on Easy Red a bit earlier, at 8:15 a.m. – 90 minutes after Charlie and other medics in the first wave. He and his team arrived aboard an LCM (Landing Craft Medium) that also carried their medical supplies, including "mortar shell casing containers and waterproofed duffle bags filled with dressings, bandages, tourniquets, sulfa powder, and plasma."[133]

Jumping from the LCM alongside the regiment's chaplain,[134] Dr. Tegtmeyer landed in chest-high water and waded ashore. The scene that confronted him was already abhorrent routine to Charlie:

> At the water's edge, floating face down with arched backs, were innumerable human forms eddying to and fro with each incoming wave, the water around them a muddy pink color. Floating equipment of all types, like flotsam and jetsam, rolled in the surf and mingled with the bodies. . . . Enemy gun[s] continued to pour artillery and machine gun fire

across the beach . . . [while] snipers and gunners picked off every head, whether officer or enlisted man, that lined up in their sights. Everywhere, the frantic cry, 'Medics! Hey medics!' was heard above the horrible din.[135]

On the beach, Tegtmeyer encountered 16th Regimental Commander Col. George Taylor, who had landed on Easy Red with his staff 15 minutes before and 50 meters west of the medical doctor and his team.[136] As Tegtmeyer recalled,

He passed us walking erect, followed by his staff and yelled for me to bring my group along. I instructed my men to follow me up to the beach and to render aid to the wounded as we passed. Crouching, running, crawling, and stumbling over the prone tightly packed bodies, we slowly worked our way up the beach, answering to the cry, 'Medic!' as we went. My men were superb as time and time again they plunged into the surf, regardless of the hail of steel fragments whistling about, to pull the wounded ashore. The wounded were hastily dressed and pulled to the shelter of the shale shelf [shingle] and left with instructions to call to the landing craft for help as they grounded. I examined scores as I went, telling the men who to dress and with whom not to bother. The number of dead – killed by mines, shell fragments, machine guns and sniper bullets – was appalling.[137]

No one knows how many men were rescued from the rising tide that morning. Nor is it known how many of them ultimately died of their wounds – or how many recovered only to be wounded or killed a few weeks or months later. What is known is how bravely and tirelessly Charlie and fellow combat medics worked to hold death at bay. Putting their incredible courage in perspective, one frontline medic who survived D-Day, as well as the battlefields in North Africa modestly remarked, "A hero's just fortunate that his maniacal resolve keeps him from becoming a casualty." [138] Although that resolve hardly saved every medic from injury, such total focus on the urgency and immediacy of their work distracted them from fear. Pfc. Waldo Werft, a combat-experienced medic who came ashore with Maj. Tegtmeyer, commented that Omaha Beach was "far worse" than what he experienced in the amphibious landing on Sicily, yet he didn't recall being as scared on D-Day as he had been in the earlier invasion. Trying to clarify, he added, "Maybe that was because it wasn't my first combat, and I was so busy treating the wounded." Then, revealing the coexistence of contraries – valor and terror – he admitted, "Let's face it, I was scared all the time but able to do my job in spite of the constant fear!"[139]

After more than two hours on the beach, at around 10:40 a.m., Werft and another dozen members of Tegtmeyer's medical section "followed the rifle companies off the beach and set up an aid station near the Regimental Command Post, dug into the seaward slope of the bluff, which sheltered them from direct enemy fire."[140]

One of the most remarkable feats typifying medics who served on the beach that day was how many of them kept working even after being wounded themselves. In Charlie's battalion, one "unusually large" medic "made three trips across the beach, carrying men on his back or in his arms" before he himself took a hit in the leg. Ignoring his injury, this medic "crawled out" to rescue a private struck down while crossing the mine strip just beyond the shingle. Somehow, he managed to hoist him onto his back and carry him to the embankment.[141] Charlie's friend "Sticks" was among those injured medics who were treated at an aid station and then went back to work. Weeks later, both medics were awarded a Purple Heart.

A particularly poignant example of a wounded medic continuing to work is Charlie's staff sergeant Ray Lambert, in charge of aid men in the 2nd Battalion's medical platoon. Lambert had been wounded previously during combat operations in Tunisia and Sicily. Lucky to be alive, he came ashore on D-Day bearing bodily scars – and perhaps more ready than ever to save others from the final fate he had barely missed. So much went wrong, yet he endured. First, recalled Lambert, while motoring shoreward early that morning and coming within a kilometer of the beach, "you could hear the machine-gun bullets hitting off the front ramp of the boat. The ramp went down, and we were in water over our heads. Some of the men drowned. Some got hit by the bullets. The boat next to ours blew up. Some of those men caught fire. We never saw them again."[142] Not only men, but also vital supplies were lost before reaching the beach, for a Jeep carrying Lambert's medical chests and the rest of his gear sunk into the deep.[143]

Then, while pushing ashore through the water, SSgt. Lambert saw wounded soldiers weighted down by their heavy equipment and unable to swim. He dragged one to the beach and then returned to haul two more out of the surf: "One guy was laying at the water's edge, his left arm hanging only by the skin. [He was] grasping in vain at his nearly severed arm as it floated in and out with the rolling tide." Having suffered injuries himself, the medical sergeant tried to console the doomed young man: "He died when I was holding his arm."[144] Lambert's first thought upon reaching the beach is seared in his memory: "'I said to one of my men, *If there's a hell, this has got to be it.*' And it was about a minute later that he got a bullet in his head." Ultimately, he said, "'only seven of the 31 men on my boat made it to the beach,'"[145] and four of those were wounded.

While Lambert was tending another soldier, a piece of shrapnel, or perhaps a bullet, pierced his own right upper arm. Nonetheless, he persisted, driven by the sheer number of troops needing care. Beyond treating casualties, he was struggling to locate and organize litter bearers and some of the remaining medics under his charge to set up the 2nd Battalion aid station. Reflecting on that dreadful morning, he said, "There were wounded all over the place. I thought, *this is impossible. How can we take care of all these men?*" Soon, "so many corpses covered the beach that the [landing] craft were having difficulty discharging their men and equipment." [146] Obviously, this "was very bad for morale, with the guys coming in from the other boats."[147]

Soon, the medical sergeant himself took a second serious hit, this one gashing his left thigh. Knocked down by the blow and bleeding profusely, he injected himself with morphine and wrapped a tourniquet as best he could with his one good arm.[148] "Pain could be endured or handled – a combination of shock and morphine helped . . . – but loss of blood could not."[149]

Struggling to remain conscious, Lambert turned to a corporal in his medical platoon, 26-year-old Raymond Lepore from Revere, Massachusetts, and instructed him to take command: "'I'm not going to make it much longer. . . . You better try to get the men together and see what you can do about treating some of these guys.'"[150] A moment later, a bullet slammed into the Italian-American medic's head, just below his helmet, and the intended replacement fell against Lambert's shoulder.[151] Then, the severely-wounded sergeant himself went into shock and passed out.[152]

There is yet more heroic drama to Lambert's story. That same morning, his older brother Bill, a staff sergeant with the 2nd Battalion's G Company on Easy Red, was also severely injured. Like Ray, Bill had earlier served as a Big Red One combat medic in North Africa and Sicily. When Bill "went down with massive wounds to his right arm and leg, his comrades stacked corpses around him to shield him from the withering fire."[153]

Medics, identified by a Red Cross symbol on their white *brassards* (armbands) and often on their helmets, were protected by the Conventions of Geneva, yet many became casualties on D-Day. Would a German machine gunner strafing the beach from a high bluff through a haze of battle smoke be able to see that the young tribesman a few hundred meters away was an unarmed first-aid man? Would a sniper pull the trigger on a medic? Charlie did not ponder such questions: "My only feeling was that I had to do what I was trained to do – help the men as much as I could. I didn't have any feelings about being killed. I didn't think about that."[154]

CHAPTER 20
Breakthrough on Easy Red

Making it alive from boat to beach required more guts and toughness than anyone could have fathomed. Every American soldier, no matter age or rank, grasped the monstrous danger of reaching the shelter of the shingle at the high-water edge of the beach. Once there, they quickly gleaned that it would take at least as much nerve to go "over the top," cut through coiled barbed wire, cross the upper beach littered with *Schrapnellminen* ("Bouncing Betties") or other hidden explosives and then climb the steep, heavily-defended bluffs.

While unyielding enemy fire from the German bunker complex WN-62 kept Charlie's comrades in Fox Company's 3rd Platoon pinned down behind the embankment near the western edge of Omaha's Fox Green sector, he continued risking all to aid wounded men within reach. Just west of him, his company commander, Captain Finke, was in the same predicament with survivors from his Headquarters boat. Three other F Company platoons were stuck behind the shingle along the middle of Fox Green. Well west of all of them, troops in F Company's 1st Platoon faced the unnerving fact that theirs was the only unit from the company to land near its designated spot on Omaha's Easy Red sector. Compounding the problem, half of that isolated platoon had not even made it to the shingle.

Exhausted and shocked by the terror, Finke's scattered troops were suspended in action, with nowhere to go. Hours would pass before they were relieved of their major combat mission that morning, which was to conquer the very strongpoint that had them cornered. Like other strongpoints placed strategically in the bluffs along Omaha Beach, WN-62's bunker complex guarded a natural valley or "draw" through which American tanks and other armored vehicles, as well as heavy artillery, could be routed inland in support of infantry platoons on the attack.

Not far west of Fox Company's 1st Platoon, the one Easy Company platoon that had also managed to land on Easy Red hunkered down behind the shingle a few hundred yards east of its scheduled spot on that beach sector. Commanded by Lt. John Spalding, men in this unit found themselves just below the ruins of a beach house that Germans had recently leveled to open a line of sight. For American infantrymen, the low stone walls that remained provided an identifiable orientation point, which they nicknamed the "Roman ruin."

A barrier of concertina wire (coiled barbed wire) between the shingle and the bluffs thwarted any forward movement, as did ongoing enemy fire. One of Spalding's sergeants tried to solve the problem with a bangalore torpedo, consisting of several connected metal tubes loaded with an explosive charge. In the face of "heavy enemy rifle, machine gun and artillery fire," he crawled across the shingle and blasted a wide gap in the wire. "He then led his [squad] through this gap . . . and through the minefield beyond the wire."[155] Armed with M1 carbines, bayonets, grenades and bazookas, the rest of the platoon also forged ahead. As Spalding recalled, "The first place we stopped was at the demolished building; there was some brush around. We were halted there by a minefield at the first slope." Referring to Charlie's comrades in Fox Company, Spalding noted that while rushing toward the ruin, "On our left we had by-passed a pillbox [WN-62], from which MG [machine-gun] fire was coming and mowing down F Co people a few hundred yards to our left [east]. There was nothing we could do to help them."[156]

Then, Spalding's platoon sergeant Philip Streczyk spotted a track between minefields.[157] It led to a barely visible trail that meandered up to the top of the bluff. A former truck driver from New Jersey, described by one of his comrades as "a little Polack," Streczyk already had three Silver Stars to his credit, one for "dauntless courage" demonstrated against Rommel's German troops in Tunisia and two more for "fearlessly proceeding over terrain swept by intense hostile machine gun fire" and "brilliant tactics and courage" in Sicily.[158] Now, echoing that earlier heroism, the 25-year-old platoon sergeant moved stealthily up the trail midway between the German bunker complexes guarding the valleys or draws codenamed E-1 (vallée du Ruquet) and E-3 (vallée du ruisseau des Moulins). Heading the platoon, Streczyk surprised a machine gunner who had been strafing the beach below. Holding him at gunpoint, the fiery sergeant couldn't believe his ears when the startled soldier pleaded nervously for his life in Polish! Bewildered, Streczyk castigated his terrified captive in their native tongue and then took a swing at him. Describing this enemy gunner, Pfc. Vincent ("Vinnie") DiGaetano in Streczyk's platoon said:

> [He's] in a one-man foxhole and he's shooting like hell. Finally, we get around behind him. He only threw up his hands when we got behind him and put a gun to his head. That's when [Streczyk] found out he was Polish . . . Streczyk asks this Polack why they shouldn't shoot him on the spot. The guy says, 'I got captured, I don't want to shoot!' . . . Hell, the SOB [son of a bitch] hit three of our guys. I hate to think how many guys he woulda hit if he was aiming! [So] Streczyk keeps talking to him in Polish and says he doesn't believe the guy. Streczyk whacked the prisoner on the back of the head and yelled, "So why the hell are you shooting at us?"

The gunner was scared out of his wits . . . Streczyk was boiling mad.[159]

Commenting on his sergeant's "tough interview," a rifleman in the squad noted it yielded results:

> The Polish gunner explained he was captured by the Germans and forced to fight against his will. He said that there were 16 Germans in a trench to the rear of his machine gun. These Germans had told their Polish prisoners that morning that they had to hold the beach no matter what. The Germans said they would shoot them in the back if the Polish didn't seem to be trying to fight. After the interview, we decided to go find those 16 Germans in the trench.[160]

At this crucial moment in the first penetration, effected midway between German strongpoints where enemy defenses were weak, military reinforcement was on the way – the beleaguered remnants of second-wave assault troops from the 16th Regiment's G Company. Under the command of Capt. Joe Dawson, its platoons had landed on Easy Red at 7 a.m. Seconds after Dawson and two of his men leaped out of their LCVP, an artillery shell struck and killed or wounded all who were still aboard. Spared that awful fate, the three lucky survivors made it to the shingle.[161]

Nearly half (63) of the men in G Company's other five platoons became casualties between boat and beach.[162] Among the seriously injured was Ray Lambert's brother SSgt. Euel W. "Bill" Lambert. Some had sought cover behind German obstacles on the tidal flat, unaware that the combat engineers had not yet completed clearing the lanes for the tanks. Consequently, according to Dawson, "They were blown by our own explosives."[163] Among the combat engineers active on Omaha were a few American Indians, including a Lummi, Navajo, Onondaga and Yuchi.[164] Facing enemy fire while hastening to detonate mines and blast 45-

meter gaps in the anti-landing obstacles, hundreds of men in various engineer combat battalions became casualties that morning.[165]

When Capt. Dawson and what remained of his troops reached the shingle, they found what he later described as a scene of "complete confusion" with misplaced, mixed up units from different companies lined up along that natural barrier, "bunched shoulder to shoulder," "huddling on patches of ground which gave them partial cover from fire," and "taking no steps against the enemy." Committed to leading his men up the bluffs to carry out their mission of capturing the nearby seacoast town of Colleville, Dawson marshalled some sanity amid the chaos. He commanded his squads to position their machine guns atop the shingle, their mortars at its base, and take high aim at the German positions on the bluff. Precisely at that moment, another wave of landing boats arrived and the enemy suddenly shifted their fire from the shingle to the surf. That narrow window of time gave Dawson's demolition and wire-cutting teams the chance to charge several yards beyond the shingle and breach a gap through the wire.[166]

Dawson and his men then scrambled across the shingle toward the minefield stretching toward the base of the dunes. There, spotting two American soldiers who had been blown up, "the men of 'G' went through the field over the bodies of the two dead men, figuring that this was their safest route."[167] Three American Indian warriors under Dawson's command joined this charge: Pfc. Nelson Tonegates (a 22-year-old northern Ute from the Rocky Mountains), Pfc. Alejandro Fragua (a 22-year old Jemez Pueblo from New Mexico) and Pvt. Nicholas Naganashe (a 21-year-old Odawa rifleman from Burt Lake, Michigan). For the Odawa warrior, this was his first and last day in combat, as he was wounded and killed in fighting later in the day.[168]

Hustling forward, they followed Lt. Spalding's platoon on the steep trail to the top of the bluff.

"We were on top of the hill by 0900," Spalding recounted. "Advanced cautiously. We were the first platoon of the 16th to hit the top. Now I ha[d] 21-22 men in my section."[169] Moving westward, Sgt. Streczyk and his squad prowled toward the German fortification WN-64 domineering the Easy Red section of the beach and the E-1 draw (Ruquet valley) leading up to Saint-Laurent. Attacking this strongpoint "with its maze of underground shelters, trenches, and dugouts," they encountered "extremely strong resistance" but successfully "cornered about twenty men and an officer. Again, there was a close firefight in the confined trenches until the enemy was overpowered and surrendered."[170] DiGaetano delivered a deathblow with a 68-pound flamethrower. Used to clear bunkers and fortified positions, this fire-spitting weapon projects a stream of flammable liquid (jellied gasoline), incinerating targets some 20-40 meters away. In DiGaetano's words: "We got the flamethrower and went to a pillbox. The Germans come out, Aaaaah! They didn't even know we had a frigging flamethrower. They were hiding in the back or something. If you get them, they know about it. Had to be like napalm. In 30 seconds, or a minute, all gone. The tank [cylinder with flammable liquid] was empty. Goodbye!"[171]

Meanwhile, at 7:40 a.m., the 16th Regiment's Alpha Company had landed at its targeted spot on Easy Red, not far west from where Lt. Spalding and Capt. Dawson had come ashore. Most of its men made it to the shingle just east of the E-1 draw (the Ruquet valley) that leads to Saint-Laurent. At 8:30 they managed to blast a large gap through the concertina wire behind the shingle there. One soldier later described what happened as they maneuvered inland:

One of my friends was a Chippewa Indian kid from northern Michigan we called Chippy. . . .[172] I followed him in [and] when we . . . got across the beach and started to move uphill towards the bluffs; he turned left, and I went straight. We hadn't gone far when he stepped on a mine. His pack was loaded with bazooka rounds and they lay all around him, and I thought they might go off, so I moved away. . . . as fast as I could. [We] hollered for Babcock, our medic, and saw that [Chippy] was badly wounded in the groin. 'It's no use. . . . you just keep on going,' Chippewa said as the medic arrived. Later that day Babcock told [us] that Chippewa had been seriously wounded, but he had a good chance of surviving if they could get him to a hospital ship in time.[173]

Miraculously, with the care of medics, this 23-year-old warrior, Pvt. Ernest D. Chippewa of the Grand Traverse Band of Ottawa & Chippewa, survived.

By this time, about 8 a.m., the 16th Regiment's 47-year-old commander Col. George Taylor had come ashore near the center of Easy Red. Just before landing, Taylor, had seen the landing craft just ahead of his take a direct hit that killed 35 men on board. Leaping from his LCVP, he had waded hastily through the incoming tide and then crawled between scattered bodies across the sand to the shingle. Quickly, he assessed the scene: A crowd of cowering soldiers from different regiments and companies were jammed behind the shingle and, sooner or later, they would be wounded or killed there by exploding artillery shells or a sniper bullet. Disoriented, many had lost their units and leaders.

Soon after 9 a.m., having captured a foothold on the high bluff, Sgt. Streczyk ignited a smoke grenade signaling the breakthrough on Easy Red. The billow of yellow-colored vapor was clearly visible from a great distance to most of the ever-growing number of soldiers gathering behind the long embankment on the beach below.

When news of the breakthrough on Easy Red reached the 16[174] Regiment's intelligence officer[174] prone behind the shingle, he immediately saw its strategic significance and ordered Cpl. Samuel Fuller to find and inform Col. Taylor. [175] (While serving in Tunisia, Fuller, a Russian-American screenplay writer, had caught the attention of Taylor who made him the "official regimental historian." Fuller had landed on Easy Red in the same boat as the 16th Regiment's Medical Detachment commander, Maj. Tegtmeyer.) Springing into action as runner, the 30-year-old corporal "moved along one hundred yards of open beach, under constant heavy fire by the enemy."[176] In his words:

> Without a moment's hesitation, I jumped up and ran back toward the landing craft, desperately searching for any sign of the colonel and what was left of our command post. Being vertical on Omaha was an invitation to death. God, how I ran! The dead and the wounded lay everywhere, body parts strewn across the sand. Scurrying like a mad rabbit, I jumped over all the corpses. I stumbled once on somebody's leg and fell onto a dead dogface [soldier]. Getting up, I careened into the surf, but floating bodies blocked me. Swerving from the water to the sand and back again, I ran until I thought my heart would burst. I fell again, got up, and fell once more, this time landing on my face between a dead medic and a bandaged soldier, the one-eyed dogface staring at me as I gasped for air. The thought of just staying there and acting like a corpse crossed my mind. [Then I] spotted him thirty feet up the beach, hugging another seawall with a captain. I scurried over to them and flopped down on my belly. Miraculously, there were no bullets in me.

Yelling over the noise, Cpl. Fuller informed the colonel that a gap had been blown open. Then, Fuller witnessed a pivotal moment in Operation Neptune:

Taylor stood up. I couldn't believe it. He just stood up. Like me, everyone who saw him get to his feet thought he'd gone nuts. 'There are two kinds of men out here!' shouted the colonel to anyone listening. 'The dead! And those who are about to die! So let's get the hell off this beach and at least die inland!' [Walking erect and boldly behind the shingle, the regimental commander] went from man to man, kicking and cursing every living dogface in his path, ordering them to get on their feet and get their asses into motion. He looked at me. 'We'll follow you, Fuller, back to the breach!' [The] sight of Colonel Taylor running up the beach inspired everyone who was still breathing to follow him. After fifty yards, Taylor no longer had to order men to their feet. Dazed dogfaces forced themselves to get up and move up the beach behind the colonel toward the only exit from that death trap. Many were hit [in a hail of bullets] and fell backward on the sand…. In single file, we got through the breach in the barbed wire and off that goddamned beach.[177]

Colonel Taylor's rallying cry also reached the fourteen first-wave survivors in Fox Company's 1st Platoon near the east end of Easy Red. They were positioned about 400-500 meters from the spot where Lt. Spalding's platoon had broken through the barbed wire and found the trail behind the Roman ruin up the bluff. The exact place and time are anyone's guess, but it was probably about 9:30 a.m. Shocked by the carnage, these men had been stuck behind the shingle for almost three hours by now.[178] Sgt. Edward Zukowski, known as "Big Zuk," had assumed charge of the troops in this decimated unit after learning that their platoon commander, Lt. Dennstedt, was dead in the water. As a 28-year-old combat veteran who had been wounded in Tunisia and awarded a Silver Star, he was up to the task – all the more so after he saw their colonel's inspiring display of bold leadership and learned that an opening had been made in the coiled wire. The fighters from this radically-reduced platoon left their wounded and dead behind and followed their courageous sergeant. As Zuk later recalled:

> I did get my men moving once the wire was breached. An opening was made for the men to get through. I told them to move forward, get into the beach grass and hold while I tried to round up more men. Many were still pinned down – couldn't tell if they were killed or just plain scared to move…. It was real hell, chaos and confusion…teams all broken up…weapons and armor scattered all over the beach. Thirty percent of the men were either killed or wounded in the first hour. My [little] brother, Joe, was in the assault craft on my left. He was a mortar sergeant. I was only hoping and praying that he came out of it alive. Then my time came. As I was running forward to join my men, I thought I ran through the same opening in the barbed wire that they had. Half-way in, I set off an anti-personnel mine and almost lost both of my legs and left arm…. My platoon [medic] came down, turned me over, and administered First Aid. Treating me with sulfur powder and pills, giving me a morphine shot in the leg to reduce pain, he left me there to continue on…. As I lay there, I looked at my rifle. The sling was cut in several pieces and the rifle stock all splintered to hell. It looked like a witch's broom. I prayed a lot that day, not so much for myself, but for my brother, Joe… hoping that should he get hit, it would be instant and [he would] not suffer.[179]

At best, only part of his prayer was answered. That morning, Sgt. Joseph Zukowski, a mortar squad leader in the same assault platoon as Charlie's medic friend Morozewicz, was killed on the beach about 1,500 meters east of his older brother. Big Zuk suffered in ways he hoped his brother would be spared. Badly wounded by shrapnel, he would spend 14 hours lying on the beach, receiving little medical attention and nearly being run over by a tank. [180]

With Big Zuk out of commission, a fellow sergeant stepped in and led the remaining soldiers in their Fox Company platoon up the Roman ruin trail to the top of the bluff. [181] There they joined the remnants of G Company headed by Capt. Dawson, whose seriously decimated unit was ready to take in any able-bodied stragglers.

By about 10 a.m., Col. Taylor had established the 16th Regiment's command post just below the crest of the bluff overlooking Easy Red. From that moment on, everyone on Easy Red was "attempting to clear inland by this route despite the fact that it was being swept by machine gun, artillery, mortar, and [other] fire."[182]

Meanwhile, the main group of Easy Company – what was left of it – had been crouched behind the shingle in the middle of Fox Green with Capt. Wozenski. Some had wounds, including Pfc. N.L. Rackard, the Creek Indian soldier from Alabama, who had fought in Sicily. Like Finke's men, they had landed at the wrong spot and been trapped for hours by machine gunners and snipers shooting from the large bunker complex guarding the E-3 inland draw to Colleville. Their impossible situation had taken a sudden turn when Wozenski noticed Streczyk's smoke signal:

> Down off to the right [west] there, maybe a thousand yards or so, I saw a yellow smoke flare. . .. and I said, I'll try to assemble as many people, alive ones, as I can, move down to a point, about [opposite] where I thought that yellow smoke flare went off, and make a move up [the bluff from] there. Because somebody got up there and I knew that I couldn't get up where I was. So I took my trench knife, and press[ed] it in peoples' backs to see if they were alive. If they were alive, I'd kick 'em or roll 'em over and say, 'Let's go!' But I didn't realize that

terror could be so great that a man, a live man, would not turn around to see who was sticking a knife into him. [It] dawned on me, after I checked two or three, that some of them were alive but they wouldn't turn around, just absolute terror. [183]

Captain Wozenski was able to rally only fourteen men still capable of fighting, ten of whom were survivors from the platoon with which he had come ashore. Crawling behind the shingle toward the Roman ruin that marked the area where they could run across the beach and climb the part of the bluff now in American hands, he and his small band were protected by an unexpected screen of billowing dark smoke. As he later recalled:

That lateral movement would have been impossible if it wasn't for the development of this battle smoke that began to cover the area. There were some tanks burning, some landing craft caught fire, and the general smoke and haze of a battlefield began to develop. This gave us enough masking so that we could get up the [bluff]. It never would have happened if we didn't have that smoke, that battlefield smoke.[184]

By the time Wozenski and his men reached the top of the bluff overlooking Easy Red, it was 10:45 a.m. He had left the USS *Henrico* just seven hours earlier with 180 men and eight officers: "I think that we had 52 killed and 54 wounded, [so] we lost about two thirds of the company in one fell swoop."[185] Now, counting heads, he had just 13 men and one fellow officer. Stunningly, only one soldier among them had a weapon that could actually fire – a carbine: "So we put that man on guard and the rest of us sat down [on the ridge where the American cemetery now stands] and cleaned our weapons."[186]

Now, men from three companies of the 16th Regiment had climbed the Roman ruin trail to the top of the bluff between the two draws – E and G company commanders with their battered survivors and a leaderless remnant of fighters from Fox Company's 1st Platoon. With WN-64 already taken out by Spalding's men, they had a foothold on the bluff and set their sights on mopping up snipers and clearing pockets of resistance between Colleville and Saint-Laurent. In the next hour or two, a skeleton force of the 16th Regiment's 2nd Battalion fought the enemy in the *bocage*, farm fields enclosed by hedgerows – earth walls overgrown with shrub and trees.

By late morning, most of the enemies on the high terrain between E-1 and E-3 draws had been routed, killed or captured. Later, a wounded Easy Company soldier still on the beach below spotted Sgt. Streczyk "coming back down the hill with a bunch of prisoners of war. They were Polish prisoners and he was kicking them in the ass and talking to them in Polack – wanted to know why they fought so hard. He was really raising hell with them."[187]

Polish captives were not unique, for American troops storming the bluffs found themselves fighting not only against German nationals such as Heinrich Severloh in the enemy's 352nd Infantry Division, but also against many Eastern Europeans in the 726th Infantry Regiment – Poles, Russian Cossacks, Georgians, Turkmen and others. Some were put to immediate good use: When Capt. Dawson sent one of his sergeants back to the beach to muster stragglers up the bluffs, the squad leader returned to the ridgetop with four men. Moving inland, he saw a German sign for *Minen* (land mines). Guided by one of the Russians captured on the bluff, they maneuvered their way through the minefield safely and "crawled on to the hedgerow beyond the field."[188]

Just as the German Wehrmacht defending Normandy featured an ethnic diversity of Germans and other nationalities, the invading Americans represented a complex ethnic mosaic that included dozens of immigrant and minority groups. Among them were first generation Italian, Ukrainian, Polish, Czech and German immigrants, plus hundreds of American Indians from scores of tribal nations.

As for the Penobscot medic, he continued pouring his youthful energy into treating the wounded within and beyond his own platoon. What was left of that platoon remained stuck behind the shingle with Lt. Rollins, just east of Capt. Finke and his reduced Headquarters unit – and some 600 meters east of the breach leading to the Roman ruin trail. Battlefield haze had kept them from seeing Streczyk's smoke signal. Since Fox Company's communication equipment had been damaged or lost, Capt. Finke had no contact with his other four platoons and could not take action on his primary mission to knock out the German stronghold keeping him and his men under fire. He knew that his battalion commander Lt. Col. Hicks and Regimental Commander Col. Taylor had been scheduled to come ashore in the middle of Easy Red. Forced to a standstill and unwilling to order his remaining fighters into a suicide attack against WN-62, the commander of Fox Company had dispatched a runner westward to find one of them and convey his untenable situation.

CHAPTER 21
Annihilation of Fox Company

In the pandemonium of Omaha Beach, Charlie began to lose track of his own platoon as he moved from one bleeding soldier to another. Survivors in his unit remained huddled behind a stretch of shingle on western Fox Green with their commanding officer, Lt. Gilbert Rollins. Immediately to their right, they could see their company commander, Capt. Finke, surrounded by the troops that had made it ashore from his landing craft. Finke suspected that his other four Fox Company platoons had also reached the protective pile of pebbles that ran the eastern length of Omaha's high-tide line. But due to water-damaged or lost radios he could not contact platoons 2, 4 and 5 and did not know they had landed about 500-750 meters to his left, while the 1st Platoon had come in on Easy Red, a few hundred meters to his right. Nor did he have any idea that the soldiers in these battered platoons had lost all their lieutenants and numerous sergeants.

Yet, by about 9:30 a.m., able-bodied remnants of Fox Company's 1st Platoon had been ordered into action by Sgt. Edward Zukowski who had assumed charge of his unit when Colonel Taylor rallied the troops. Leaving their dead and wounded on Easy Red, they had moved toward the Roman ruin and climbed the steep footpath blazed by Sgt. Streczyk earlier that morning. "Big Zuk" had stepped on a landmine, but thirteen of his men had made it to the top of the bluff. Once there, they had joined the remaining troops of G Company, commanded by Capt. Joe Dawson.

Since the colonel's orders did not reach the men beyond Easy Red, Capt. Finke knew nothing of the breakout about 600 meters to his right. What he did know was that he and Lt. Rollins together had just twenty men fit enough to fight and that there was still no apparent way to advance this reduced force from their besieged position directly under the guns of WN-62. Having no contact with four of his six platoons, nor with his superior officers, Finke waited impatiently for his platoon runner to return with information from 2nd Battalion commander Lt. Col. Herbert Hicks. Anxious for action after being stuck for so long, some of his men had to be reminded of enemy snipers. As Pvt. Funkhouser recalled, Sgt. Lombarski "jumped up and emptied his rifle one time and Captain Finke told him to stay down," telling him the obvious: "'You're not doing any good.'" Nonetheless, "about six men were wounded by sniper fire at this position."[189] For the time being, the captain could do little more than press his men to hold tight in the shortening shadow of the shingle.

The twin enemies of withering German fire power and a wild sea had taken a ghastly toll, and gains were too small and too few to rouse hope. It was not just that American fighting forces had been swept off course, missed their landing sites and suffered countless casualties. Radio equipment had been damaged or lost, a dozen landing boats had been wrecked and a "tremendous tonnage of tanks, half-tracks, M-7s [105 mm Howitzer Motor Carriages], jeeps, trucks, and other vehicles [had] sunk, [and] others were destroyed..."[190] Not counting the wounded, this beach had already exacted many hundreds of lives, with "a majority of the casualties . . . taken in the first hour."[191]

Amid this slaughter, combat engineers continued blowing up anti-boat obstacles on the tidal flat to clear the way for incoming waves of landing craft disgorging troops on Easy Red. More soldiers. More casualties. "Congestion grew dangerous. Shoulder to shoulder, men lay prone on the pebbles, stones, shale. Some lay half in the water."[192] Half a dozen Sherman tanks had made it to the beach and also a few bulldozers, but almost all the others had sunk.[193]

So dire was the situation at that point that General Omar Bradley, commander in chief of the American ground forces, later admitted: "From the few radio messages that we overheard and the firsthand reports of observers in small craft reconnoitering close to shore, I gained the impression that our forces had suffered an irreversible catastrophe, that there was little hope we could force the beach. Privately, I considered evacuating the beachhead and directing the follow-up troops to Utah Beach or the British beaches."[194]

But then, the fast-rising tide that had wreaked such havoc on boats, lives and strategic plans, presented an opportunity that played a crucial role in setting the stage for averting irreversible disaster. About 10 a.m., aware that by flood tide fifty minutes later the sea would have risen more than six meters since the landings began, a navy admiral directed a squadron of six destroyers to move shoreward in support of the beleaguered infantry.[195] Each of these swift warships, 106 meters long with drafts less than 3.6 meters deep, had to be navigated through a scramble of smaller boats. Maneuvering parallel to the beach only 800 meters off the high-water line, and sometimes even much closer, fully exposed them to shelling from German artillery. But each destroyer came equipped with a mighty arsenal that included four 138-caliber guns with a range of about 10 kilometers and capable of firing 22 rounds a minute. In the course of an hour, beginning at 10:15, they would unleash a broadside firestorm of 500-1,000 rounds of 127 mm (5-inch) shells on German strongpoints, knocking out anti-tank guns and demolishing bunkers.[196]

During this time, assault platoons of the Big Red One's 18th Infantry Regiment and the 115th Regiment of the Blue and Grey Division (29th) waded ashore at the junction of Omaha's Easy Red and Easy Green sectors – between the Ruquet valley (E-1) and Les Moulins (D-3), draws that both led to Saint- Laurent.[197] Several American Indian warriors formed part of these fighting units – a Kumeyaay, Navajo, Potawatomi, Oglala Lakota and Shoshone-Paiute in the 18th [198] and a Tuscarora, Navajo, Jicarilla Apache and northern Ute in the 115th, along with Passamaquoddy combat medic from seacoast Maine, Pvt. Phillip Neptin. The first elements of the 32nd Field Artillery Battalion, which supported the 18th Regiment, also landed on Easy Red about 10.30 a.m. This battalion included American Indian artillerymen, some serving as forward observers. Among them was an Anishinaabe from the White Earth reservation[199] and two Lakota, including a Sicangu Lakota from the Rosebud reservation – coincidentally named Anthony Omaha Boy.[200]

Meanwhile, the 2nd Battalion assault troops of the 16th Regiment's E and G Companies had climbed up the Roman ruin trail and captured WN-64 on the east side of the Ruquet valley (E-1), but its companion strongpoint WN-65 on the opposite side of that valley remained in enemy hands. Its elimination was urgent, so American tanks and other armored vehicles could roll inland from the beach and control the coastal road linking Colleville and Saint-Laurent. Action toward that end came with the arrival of flood tide at 10:50 a.m. when one of the navy destroyers steered close to the beach and took aim at WN-65. The ship's gunner could not actually see the well-camouflaged German position, but he took his cue from a crippled Sherman tank that was targeting the thick concrete bunker with firepower insufficient to seriously damage the enemy stronghold.[201] Thus aided by the tank gunner on the beach, the destroyer's mighty deck guns fired 127 mm (5-inch) shells at the rate of one every four seconds directly over the heads of the men on Easy Red. Around 11 a.m., when its fifth salvo scored a direct hit, "a large cloud of green smoke was noted and the [German] mortar battery ceased firing."[202] Next, a navy destroyer systematically pounded several camouflaged enemy machine-gun nests spotted on the bluffs near the WN-65 bunker complex and also shelled those into oblivion.[203]

The roaring thunder of these heavy guns and sight of exploding concrete galvanized soldiers who had piled up behind the shingle on Easy Red and Fox Green. An infantry platoon from the 18th climbed up the bluff, flushed some twenty dazed enemy soldiers from their badly damaged pillbox at WN-65 and took them prisoner.[204] With both German strongpoints guarding the inland draw to Saint-Laurent now captured and dozens of enemy machine guns and artillery pieces finally silenced, other troops pinned down on Easy Red could finally press forward to secure the Ruquet valley.[205] "We encountered minefields on the way up" to the high ground then being cleared of enemies by 16th Regiment troops, a company commander in the 18th Regiment's 2nd Battalion recounted, but we "made it up to the top without any problems."[206] Then orders came for his battalion to back up "the mission of the decimated 16th RCT [Regimental Combat Team] and head for Colleville."[207] So these Big Red One soldiers pressed further inland while Blue and Grey troops advanced into the valley and pushed toward Saint-Laurent, which came under siege.

By then, troops of the 146th Engineer Combat Engineers Battalion had landed with bulldozers and were opening gaps through the shingle and dunes, as well as filling the anti-tank ditches with pebbles and gravel. These combat engineer soldiers, which included a Yuchi and a Navajo,[208] also cleared a wide swath through the minefields. With the gunfire from the machine-gun nests and WN-65 silenced, the combat engineers turned the Ruquet valley (E-1 draw) into a vital artery for armored vehicles and artillery streaming inland toward Saint-Laurent and Colleville.[209]

Immediately after the shelling of strongpoint WN-65, one of the navy destroyers was ordered toward Fox Red on Omaha's eastern end. Now that the tide was going out, the crosscurrent also reversed, pulling even these small warships westward. From that eastern section of the beach, a small draw led to the village of Cabourg. After losing numerous men while storming the beach, troops of the 16th Regiment's 3rd Battalion had been trapped below this draw for hours by WN-60. Quickly, the destroyer moved into position 800 meters from the shore and took aim. The ship's action report notes what happened next:

> Observed enemy machine gun emplacement on side of steep hill at west end of beach Fox Red. . . . Fired two half [two-gun] salvos. Target destroyed. Shifted fire to casemate [bunker] at top of hill, fired two half salvos, target destroyed. Army troops begin slow advance uphill from beach. Maneuvering ship to stay in position against current which is running west at 2.8 knots.[210]

Minutes after the destroyer shelled WN-60, the 3rd Battalion attacked and skirmished with German forces entrenched on the bluff.[211] Then, fifteen surviving enemies defending the strongpoint surrendered. With this bunker complex taken out, these Big Red One troops could push inland toward the village of Cabourg, turn west on top of the ridge and attack the nearby strongpoint WN-61 positioned on the east side of the E-3 draw to Colleville from behind.[212]

Now the time for action had also come for the remnants of Fox Company platoons 2, 4 and 5, pinned down behind the shingle almost directly in front of WN-61. Surrounded by a minefield, this German defense complex included a bunker that comprised two anti-tank guns (50 mm and 88 mm) and two machine guns, along with other firepower. Like its counterpart WN-62 on the opposite side of the valley, it was buried in the side of the bluff overlooking the beach at Fox Green.

With F Company's 5th Platoon commander dead, SSgt. Raymond Strojny now assumed command. The oldest son of Polish immigrants, Strojny had been a factory worker in Taunton, Massachusetts, before entering the military at Fort Devens in early 1942. Now 24-years old, he had fought in North Africa and heroically distinguished himself in Sicily, for which he was awarded the Silver Star.[213]

Leaving behind many dead and wounded comrades, Strojny and six fellow fighters in his unit skulked eastward, away from the cross-fire stretch of beach between WN-62 and WN-61 to a better tactical position. There he set up a line of fire that took out two enemy machine gun posts. Then he spotted an 88 mm German anti-tank gun firing at three Sherman tanks from a bunker dug into the bluff's edge.[214]

Seizing a shrapnel-pierced bazooka from a dead soldier, he grabbed some rockets and ran within effective firing distance, some 250 meters from the bunker above him. He took aim at the anti-tank gun, aware that his damaged bazooka might explode and maim or kill him instantly. But it functioned, and he scored two direct hits.

Out of rockets, Strojny rushed back down to the beach, crossed over a minefield and returned to his firing position with six more rounds. These hit their mark. One ripped into the big concrete emplacement, causing the ammunition inside it to explode. An enemy sniper answered swiftly, setting his sights on Strojny and sending a bullet straight to his head. Miraculously, the heroic sergeant survived: "One bullet went through the front of his helmet, circled his head and tore out through the side near his left ear. Still the target for German fire, Strojny worked his way back for more rockets for the bazooka and again in position, finished off the first pillbox and then blasted the second into flames."[215]

Although Strojny had fired into both WN-61 pillboxes, this bunker complex still posed a grave challenge. As he led fellow Fox Company soldiers and stragglers from other decimated units up the bluffs, a few Sherman tanks trundled onto the beach below and one of the navy destroyers was signaled to shell what remained of the German strongpoint. From a ship's control tower, it was difficult to see through battlefield smoke and spot the precise location of enemy bunkers. So, as in this instance, when there was a working radio available, shore observers called in their targets by radio. Once again, warship artillery provided a vital assist. As Strojny later recalled, this particular destroyer maneuvered very close to the beach "to zero in on the hillside. . . . After the bombardment, we went into the tunnels [chasing] after the German mortar crews."[216]

Even for the brazen sergeant and his small band of Fox Company fighters, the task ahead was terrifying, for the bluffs were honeycombed with defensive trenches, machine-gun nests, sniper dugouts, tunnels and bunkers. Also, Strojny noted, enemy troops had concealed their mortars, digging them into the hill with only the ends of the steel barrels sticking out. Nonetheless, by late morning, WN-61 was also in American hands, with numerous Germans killed and more than a dozen captured.

Moving farther east, Strojny and his soldiers later joined up with remnants of their regiment's 3rd Battalion, K Company. Soldiers of Fox Company's reduced 2nd and 4th platoons, who had also lost their officers earlier in the day, ended up with the 3rd Battalion as well. (One K Company rifleman, Potawatomi tribesman Pfc. Potts from the Central Plains, heroically distinguished himself in ground combat but was captured later in the day and spent the rest of the war in a *Stalag* – German prisoner-of-war camp.)[217]

During these vanguard breakthroughs, the immobilized remnants of the two assault platoons that had come ashore with Capt. Finke and Lt. Rollins grew ever more frustrated being hemmed in by enemies spying down on them from sniper and machine-gun nests on the bluff and in the bunker complex of WN-62. Nonetheless, the Fox Company commander held on doggedly to their combat objective while waiting for his runner to return with news from 2nd Battalion commander Hicks. All morning long, they'd had just one glimmer of hope: the sight of navy destroyers shelling the German strongpoints with a vengeance. Pvt. Funkhouser in Charlie's platoon recalled: "Some of those ships came in [so close] I thought I could have hit them with a rock."[218] Sgt. Lombarski in Finke's Headquarters unit saw one of the destroyers come "within four hundred yards off shore..."[219] The USS *Doyle* came so close inshore that in addition to her heavy deck guns, even her light guns peppered the German bunkers and machine gun nests. Charlie also held vivid memories of "large artillery and small arms coming from both directions [and] allies shooting over our heads up into the bunkers."[220]

Now, the tide having turned, the sea began to recede from the shingle. Sometime around 11 a.m., Capt. Finke's runner returned from his high-risk mission[221] with an order from Hicks "to move all second battalion men to the right [west] to join the battalion" at the command post inland. At last, the hours-long deadlock was about to be broken. Anxious to finally move into action, the Fox Company commander instructed Sgt. Lombarski to rally the remaining fighters, while he quickly pushed ahead on his own. Moving stealthily behind the shingle about "600 yards to the right"[222] toward the spot on Easy Red where the first breach on the beach had occurred earlier that morning, Finke reached the Roman ruin, quickly climbed the trail and hastened toward his battalion's command post, which Lt. Col. Hicks had established in a tree grove a few hundred meters inland from Taylor's Regimental Command Post.[223]

Meanwhile, Capt. Finke's order was passed down the shingle word of mouth: "F Company moving out. You pass it on."[224] This was easier said than done, since the battered F

Company platoons to Lombarski's distant left were widely scattered, mixed up with other units and not within view. Moreover, any movement could attract enemy sniper attention. It was nearly noon by the time Lombarksi had "notified everyone possible to prepare to move."[225] Since most of the troops in his and Lt. Rollin's platoons had been killed or wounded, and he was still uninformed about the whereabouts and capacity of Fox Company's four other assault platoons, Lombarski could rally only about twenty men still fit for combat.[226] They left without Charlie.

All morning long, throughout the rapidly incoming tide, the Penobscot medic had been focused on treating wounded men along the narrowing strip of beach, gradually separating from his platoon until he was beyond reach of his company's "moving out" order. As recalled by Funkhouser of Charlie's platoon, "We got up and started down the beach [westwards] and there were bodies laying three and four across rolling with the surf back and forth, just all the way down."[227]

Sgt. Lombarski, followed by Lt. Rollins and their small band of fighters, crawled away, moving west toward Easy Red and the breakthrough point at the Roman ruin by the access point to the steep trail up the bluff. Since both German strongpoints guarding the Ruquet valley had been eliminated, this wide stretch of beach was now much less dangerous, but still far from safe. Nearing the top of the bluff, the small band of Fox Company fighters following Lombarski passed by Col. Taylor's Regimental Command Post, just 20 meters from the Regimental aid station where a group of medics worked under Maj. Tegtmeyer. Dug into the seaside slope, the aid station and command post were sheltered from enemy artillery fire from inland batteries.

Once atop the bluff, Lombarski and his men continued a few hundred meters inland until they reached the 2nd Battalion command post within sight of enemy-occupied

Colleville. There they rejoined their commander, Capt. Finke. Not far from this makeshift headquarters, Capt. Wozenski was regrouping remnants of Easy Company's platoons into an effective fighting force.[228] Among his soldiers was Rackard, the Creek Indian warrior who had earlier fought in Sicily and would be wounded before the end of the day.

Half of the twenty Fox Company men Sgt. Lombarski rallied were unable to keep up after moving away from their position behind the shingle facing WN-62. Now it seemed evident that something was preventing them from joining their comrades atop the bluff. Determined to "find the stragglers and any other F Company men he could,"[229] Finke dispatched a runner back down the now clearly demarcated trail. It turned out that Lt. Rollins and Sgt. Plona[230] had been wounded (perhaps by a sniper) "while moving forward toward the break through position" at the Roman ruin on Easy Red. And it appeared that men who were with them, most likely members of Rollins' platoon, "had been unable to stand the pace."[231]

Disintegrated and decimated, Fox Company no longer existed as a tactical unit. Confronted with this cold reality, Capt. Finke was told that he could not lead his few remaining soldiers into combat as planned to carry out the 2nd Battalion's military objective – the capture of Colleville. Instead, Lt. Col. Hicks ordered Lombarski and his ten soldiers to furnish security, providing east-flank protection for his command post since enemy snipers and forward observers were directing artillery on his fighters.

Lombarski set out to position a three-man outpost. Suddenly, from a hidden position somewhere near the Colleville draw to their east, a German machine gun opened fire on them. Acting swiftly, Capt. Finke led a small patrol to take out the enemy gunner. It was early afternoon, about

12:30. One patrol member, Funkhouser, later recounted how they moved forward through the thick hedgerows:

> I was right behind Captain Finke. Paddie Feagan was on this side and we were every 10 feet apart. . . . Captain Finke took off down that road. . . . He sent Paddie Feagan and me down in this field. I started down through there and a machine gun opened up so I hit the ground. I couldn't see anything. I started crawling forward . . . and machine guns started firing in front of me, just coming towards me like that and I hit the ground. And I did the unforgivable. I rolled [down a slope], but when I rolled I turned loose of my M-1 rifle. I don't know how far I rolled, and then I just laid there. By that time, they started dropping mortars in, the heavy 81 mm. And there was a ditch around this field, at the bottom of the hedgerow. I had my choice of trying to make that ditch or going back after my rifle and [then] trying to make the ditch, so I took the ditch. I was in that ditch and mortar was falling all around. In the meantime, Captain Finke brought the rest of the company down on that hedgerow for them to try to give us some fire support so we could get out. The mortars got too heavy and he [Finke] got hit and then they pulled back so Paddie and I were out there on our own. [We] went up along the hedge[row] and Paddie was out in the road by then. We started back towards the beach, went around the turn and I saw some of our guys [from F Company]. . . . They were in this field [now the war cemetery], dug in. I didn't have anything to dig in with and no weapon."[232]

Seriously wounded in this action and in terrible pain, Capt. Finke received treatment from a combat medic and ordered Lombarski "to take the unit on to Colleville."[233] Then, Fox Company's last standing officer limped back to his battalion command post. Easy Company commander Capt. Wozenski saw him and later recalled: "He had blood streaming down all over the side of his helmet."[234]

When Lt. Col. Hicks learned of the mortar round that wounded Finke, he decided to move the 2nd Battalion command post a few hundred meters back toward the edge of the bluff.[235] Leaving the post, Finke hobbled his way to the aid station, where Maj. Tegtmeyer was directing a small team of surgical assistants and other medics. As the regimental surgeon later wrote in his memoir:

> A trickling of prisoners passing through the C.P. [16th Regimental Command Post], the constant cover of our own fighter planes overhead, and the constant firing of our destroyers and cruisers at inland targets was reassuring even though the [inland batteries of] enemy artillery was raising hell with deadly accuracy along the beach. As the explosions continued . . . Captain John Finke came in with a compound fracture of the right arm and a wound of the right leg. Both wounds were already dressed but he needed morphine.[236]

In fact, Finke required considerably more medical attention and was later evacuated to a hospital in England.[237] Whatever victorious expectations he may have had for this day, surely, they did not include completely losing track of four of his six platoons, failing to carry out his mission and losing almost 60 percent of his troops and all of his officers. Unaware of the heroics of his combat medics remaining on the beach and fighters pressing forward on the other side of the vallée du ruisseau des Moulins (E-3 draw), Captain Finke left Omaha fearing he had nothing to show other than staggering losses. Years later, commenting on the annihilation of Fox Company, he said little more than: "My company had lost all of its officers by the time I was wounded around noon . . ."[238] In fact, it was worse, as Pvt. Funkhouser recognized: "My company was just more or less eliminated as a fighting unit. There wasn't enough of us."[239]

CHAPTER 22
Death of a Young Medic

Focused on his work and determined to help as many as he possibly could, Charlie had paid no attention to the incessant barrage of fire coming down from German stronghold WN-62. Certainly, he never even glimpsed Pvt. Heinrich Severloh, positioned in a WN-62 machine gun nest 25 meters above the beach. Entrenched about seven meters from the large bunker's artillery observation post, this brutally effective killer wreaked terror on hundreds of American soldiers struggling below him on Fox Green. Many of the wounded men Charlie treated on D-Day were victims of this 20-year-old German soldier situated about 150 meters from the shingle. That distance represented a world of difference between the Penobscot Indian medic and the German machine gunner. Yet, both young draftees, randomly placed in pitiless opposition, were facing gruesome peril in a country equally foreign to them.

For hours now, ever since daybreak, Severloh had tirelessly targeted anybody and anything that moved on the wide shore below him. He had to keep his ever-growing numbers of enemies at bay, knowing for certain, "If I don't shoot them, then one of them will shoot me." As a well-trained soldier, Severloh knew some of the basic rules of the Geneva Convention, prohibiting the killing of non-combatants. So, he had not aimed at harmless medics like Charlie as they rushed to rescue men felled by him or his comrades. Taking proper care, gunners and sharpshooters at the strong points or in the trenches on the high bluffs could usually spot a medic's conspicuous white armband with its bold Red Cross symbol. But that did not mean they didn't happen to hit medics in the haze of smoke on the beach below – or that some kill-crazy snipers gave little or no effort to avoid doing so.[240]

By early afternoon, casualties in Charlie's regiment, mixed up with those from other units, remained behind the shingle, while most of their comrades who were still fit to fight had escaped from Fox Green. About mid-afternoon, after spending hours with his finger on the trigger, an exhausted Severloh realized he was the last person still firing. As he recalled, "I could see tanks maneuvering on the beach and knew that I couldn't hold them alone. . . . I heard an order shouted by Lieutenant Frerking . . . that we should retreat." Having fired about 12,000 rounds, the young gunner leapt up to leave his post, grabbing his weapon and a 50-bullet drum. "I ran from bomb crater to bomb crater behind our bunker complex." Then, he paused briefly, waiting for his commanding officer. But in the moment since calling out his order to retreat, Frerking had been killed. So, Severloh hurried up the wooded inland draw without him. As he ran, two bullets hit him, and he threw his heavy machine gun into a bush so he could escape less encumbered. About 20 minutes later, he reached his fortified command post WN-63 on the edge of Colleville. After receiving first aid from a German medic, he was put in charge of four Americans captured just a short while earlier.[241]

With WN-62 finally silenced, the relentless rata-tat-tat of enemy machine gun fire was now coming from a kilometer or more inland, and nearby explosions of incoming artillery and mortar shells had lessened. But after being exposed to the thunderous din of artillery and machine guns for so many hours, Charlie was all but deaf to any nuances in the noise. What held his attention was the ebbing tide. The beach had widened by a few hundred meters, revealing a broad flat where hundreds of dead bodies lay crumpled among the anti-invasion obstacles, burned-out landing boats and piles of other debris. For now, the corpses were ignored because they were outnumbered by the suffering wounded – some slowly bleeding to death but still painfully conscious, others no longer aware that their lives hung in the balance.

Charlie had long ago lost contact with other Fox Company men. All too many were among the dead, others among the dozens of wounded he had treated hours earlier. The rest had simply vanished, whereto he did not know. Slowly walking eastward along the shingle, Charlie surveyed rows of soldiers too seriously hurt to fight another day. Not evacuated in time, many would not make it through the night. They had been left behind by their platoons, or what was left of them – survivors who were now fiercely pushing inland, killing, maiming and capturing enemies. Desperately fighting back, the Germans were outnumbered and outgunned by the continuous landings of new American troops, but they were not defeated.

Reaching a place many hundreds of meters east from where he had come ashore early that morning, Charlie noticed a critically wounded man lying against the shingle. To his horror, he realized it was one of his fellow medics – Eddie Morozewicz, the Polish-American kid from New Jersey. They had last seen each other on the troopship before climbing down rope nets into neighboring landing boats – Charlie in the LCVP carrying the 3rd Platoon commanded by Lt. Rollins and Eddie attached as a first aid man to the 2nd Platoon assault troops led by Lt. Rush.

Decades later, reluctant to recall that traumatic moment, Charles said simply: "On the beach I did see one medic I knew – Morozowicz. He was very seriously wounded – a stomach wound, his insides all open. He was beyond help. He was conscious."[242]

Like Charlie, Eddie had waded back into the sea to

pull injured men from the rising waters that gruesome morning. But, unlike his Indian friend, he had been gravely wounded while doing his job. The Penobscot medic guessed that a hot steel fragment from an exploding mortar shell had torn into his stomach. In excruciating pain but still aware, Morozewicz recognized Charlie as he bandaged the gaping wound as best as he could. Both knew that it made little difference. The only thing Charlie could really do for his buddy was to lessen his agony – to punch a needle into his thigh and allow the morphine to work.

Charlie stayed with Eddie for a while. Then, unable to do anything more and knowing he had to move on, he readied himself to leave. The two medics bade each other farewell, knowing that death was imminent, surely for one of them, and perhaps for both.

Thinking back on that sad moment, Charles said, "Morozewicz is the only fallen combat medic I remember seeing. Later I learned that eight medics from my regiment died during the assault. Thinking about it, the mortar fire, I'm not surprised. The fire was just sweeping back and forth. It didn't differentiate between riflemen and combat medics. It was only by the grace of God that any got through without being hit."

Charlie's medical commander, Major Tegtmeyer, who spent several hours on Easy Red that morning, inspected numerous injured and dead medics. Most were hit by mortar shells or machine guns, but, he concluded, "Many of the Aidmen wounded were shot intentionally." Declaring the Geneva Convention "a failure" (while, ironically, breaking it himself by carrying a Colt .45 despite being a doctor), the major cautioned, "The white brassard draws fire…. The Geneva Convention brassard makes the Company Aidmen's job the most hazardous in the Army."[243]

Many of the GIs seriously wounded early on at Omaha Beach, including Big Red One medics, were taken back to the landing boats that had brought them ashore. The LCVPs delivered them to the USS *Samuel Chase* and other ships that were transformed into emergency hospitals and headed swiftly across the Channel that afternoon. Hours later, a fleet of ambulances met these human wrecks at Portsmouth Harbor and raced them to hospitals for emergency surgery, including amputations.

Teams of army doctors, nurses and other medical personnel worked tirelessly to alleviate suffering and save lives. Among the many nurses were dozens of American Indian women, including the two Lakota nurses then working in England – Lt. Marcella LeBeau, caring for American soldiers injured in Normandy and brought to the 76th General Hospital, and Lt. Rose Blue Thunder, tending those carried to the 186th General Hospital. Recalling the first casualties shipped from the invasion beaches, Rose commented, "I thought I was tough, but on D-Day my own heart was wounded seeing a stream of boys in the prime of their youth, shot up, legs blown off, eyes blinded; that was a tough day for me…. I had to go in the linen closet, and I cried. We worked 12, 14, 16 hours a day caring for the wounded."[244]

Later that day, soldiers from a collecting company worked across Omaha Beach, bringing litters and blankets, caring for the wounded still waiting to be ferried to vessels that would take them to England for hospitalization. The hundreds who died on that shore were carried to a collecting point set up by a Graves Registration platoon near the west end of the beach. To that platoon fell the dismal task of removing each dead man's duplicate dog tag, saving his few personal possessions and burying him in a temporary shore-side grave. Helmets, boots, gasmasks, belts – and anything else of value – were collected for military reuse.

Litter bearers also picked up Eddie's body and the corpses of seven other medics with whom Charlie had lived and trained on the English side of the choppy sea. Few units on Normandy's five invasion beaches suffered more casualties than Fox Company. Its troop strength plummeted to 20 percent during the morning assault on Omaha Beach – the opening day of Operation Overlord. No one will ever know how many men these brave medics managed to save before they, too, went down.

Later, like thousands of other soldiers buried in temporary graves on D-Day or soon thereafter, Eddie would be reburied at the American Cemetery overlooking Omaha Beach. And six decades after that his old friend Charles would stand before the white marble cross marking his grave, pausing in contemplation before offering him a salute.

Charles visiting Eddie Morozewicz's grave at the Normandy American Cemetery for the first time, 2 October 2007. ©Harald E.L. Prins

CODA

Late in the afternoon on D-Day, Charlie's Penobscot friend Melvin Neptune waded onto the now quieted Fox Green sector of Omaha Beach. He was on his way to heroically take out a German machine gun nest. Charlie did not see him. Nor was he aware of some 500 other North American Indians who landed in Normandy on 6 June 1944 – about 175 of them on Omaha. It remains unknown how many of those 500 were wounded, captured or killed that day and night, but at least three of them perished on Omaha, six on the Cotentin Peninsula and another thirteen on Juno Beach.

Before Nazi Germany surrendered on 7 May 1945, many hundreds more tribesmen became casualties. Among them were Penobscots, including Charlie's childhood friend Pfc. Leslie Banks. This 19-year-old machine gunner was awarded a Silver Star a few months before being severely wounded by a German Tiger tank in the Battle of the Bulge. Pvt. David Lewis, another Penobscot from Indian Island, was killed while crossing the Moselle River in September 1944. And Pvt. Philip Neptin, a combat medic from the neighboring Passamaquoddy tribe, died when he stepped on a landmine just days after his D-Day landing on Omaha. The Mi'kmaq nation, too, suffered losses, including the death of Pvt. Charles Doucette from Cape Breton Island. Taken prisoner on D-Day, this father of four was executed by German SS troops just outside Caen the following day.

But a far greater number of North American Indians survived, including Melvin. Charlie's three brothers, two of whom served in the Pacific, also made it home. Florence Nicolar Shay did not become a Gold Star Mother. Her prayers were answered.

As authors of this book, we are grateful that our friend Charles agreed to share his D-Day experiences so we could draw attention to the sacrifices of so many other forgotten or ignored North American Indians who also helped liberate European nations suffering under foreign military occupation.

Pvt. Charles Shay, Platoon Medic, F. Company, 16th Infantry Regiment, outside Aachen, Germany, about 140 days after D-Day. Taken by an unknown fellow soldier, this photo was probably sent home to Charlie's mother. Courtesy Charles N. Shay.

END NOTES

End notes and sources indicated throughout this text will appear in our forthcoming full-length biography of Charles Shay. Notably, almost all quotes from Charles come from interviews with the authors carried out since 1998.

59674697R00076

Made in the USA
Columbia, SC
06 June 2019